# WELFARE'S END

# GWENDOLYN MINK

# WELFARE'S END

Cornell University Press

ITHACA AND LONDON

First published 1998 by Cornell University Press
First printing, Cornell Paperbacks, 2002

Printed in the United States of America

Library of Congress Cataloging-in-Publication Data

Mink, Gwendolyn, 1952–
Welfare's end / Gwendolyn Mink
p.   cm.
Includes bibliographical references and index.
ISBN 0-8014-3347-9 (cloth : alk. paper).
ISBN 0-8014-8393-X (pbk. : alk. paper).
1. Unmarried mothers—Government policy—United States.
2. Poor mothers—Government policy—United States.
3. Welfare recipients—United States.
4. Public welfare—United States.
5. Public welfare—United States—History—20th century.
6. United States—Social policy I. Title
HV700.5.M56   1998
362.83'928'0973—dc21          97-38838

Cornell University Press strives to use environmentally responsible suppliers and
materials to the fullest extent possible in the publishing of its books. Such
materials include vegetable-based, low-VOC inks and acid-free papers that are either
recycled, totally chlorine-free, or partly composed of nonwood fibers. Books that
bear the logo of the FSC (Forest Stewardship Council) use paper taken from forests
that have been inspected and certified as meeting the highest standards for
environmental and social responsibility. For further information, visit our website at
www.cornellpress.cornell.edu.

5   6   7   8   9   10      Cloth printing

1   2   3   4   5   6   7   8   9   10      Paperback printing

for my parents,
John Francis Mink and
Patsy Takemoto Mink

# Contents

# Preface

I n 1993, as I was completing a book on Progressive Era and New Deal social policy innovations affecting women, Bill Clinton was preparing his plan to end welfare. My historical research and analysis of mother-directed policy had prepared me to tackle contemporary welfare issues, but it was my political despair at President Clinton's calculated deployment of welfare reform against poor single mothers that spurred me to shift my scholarly attention from the mistakes made by welfare's early twentieth-century proponents to the outrages perpetrated by its late twentieth-century foes. As this book began to take shape in my mind, the Republicans rode to power in Congress with promises to end welfare even more swiftly and brutally than Bill Clinton had planned. My scholarly and political lives fully fused, I spent much of the next two years battling Republican welfare reform.

As a steering committee member (and later co-chair) of the Women's Committee of One Hundred, I worked closely and daily with feminist scholars and activists in a campaign to derail the Republican initiative. From the Committee's founder, Eva Feder Kittay; from my sister co-chairs, Guida West and

Ruth Brandwein; from steering committee members who gave up hours to discuss policy and strategy in conference calls; from committee members with whom I joined to lobby senators and representatives; and from my mother, arguably our staunchest supporter in Congress—from all these women I learned much about welfare, about politics, and about commitment in the face of adversity.

Our campaign against the Republican welfare initiative focused my attention on the relationship between welfare rights and women's equality. Our failure to make reliable allies of the five white Democratic women in the Senate and of most white Democratic women in the House of Representatives also reminded me that feminists do not always act in the interests of other women. Out of these concerns—with welfare and equality, and with welfare reform and feminism—emerged my resolve first to illuminate the unique inequalities endured by poor single mothers in welfare law and then to suggest what welfare justice could look like if we made poor single mothers' equality as citizens and as women our priority.

Although most of its members will no doubt find many of my ideas wacky, impractical, or just plain wrong, the Women's Committee of One Hundred is part of this book, for I have benefited enormously from being one of them. My mother, Patsy Takemoto Mink, is also part of this book, not only because she read and commented on every word (or so it seemed) but also because her own legislative struggles to stop the Republican wrecking ball profoundly influenced my assessments of policy and political possibilities. I also owe special thanks to Laura Efurd, on whom I could always depend for a clear answer to my confusing questions about the status of legislation or about cryptic statutory provisions.

Seminal conversations with Dana Frank and Anne Kornhauser emboldened my thinking about welfare and inequality. As friends and interlocutors, they were indispensable to the early development of this book. Kereth Frankel Klein's legal research and Jessica Delgado's policy sleuthing yielded invaluable tools for this analysis. Jessica's assistance made Chapter 2 relatively easy to write. Keri's made Chapter 3 more difficult than I had anticipated, but also more fun.

Eileen Boris and Felicia Kornbluh bravely agreed to review the manuscript, piece by piece, for Cornell University Press. They vetted each chapter swiftly and thoroughly—so thoroughly I sometimes wondered whether I could possibly accommodate everything they had to say. I absorbed as much of their brilliant and erudite feedback as I could manage; and while they of course do not bear any responsibility for the final product, I am sure that *Welfare's End* is a better book because of their contributions to it.

Out of the goodness of their hearts, Theodore J. Lowi and Wally Goldfrank read each chapter as I wrote it. I have come to rely on Wally's unfiltered editorial criticism and on his pithy insights, as well as on his honesty when something I've written "doesn't sing." I have entered a state of permanent indebtedness to Ted, whose unstinting reviews of each chapter gave me lots to think about and lots to revise. More than my chief critic, he generously offered alternative language and more precise formulations when words failed me. His cautious praise, meanwhile, kept me optimistic, but humble. He, too, is in this book; in fact, his early enthusiasm for its core arguments gave me the confidence to begin writing it, and his sustained interest fueled me to press on.

At Cornell University Press, Peter Agree gets all the credit for enabling me to write another book. His arrangement with reviewers, his sense of just how often and how far to nudge me toward completion, and his timely recommendations of mostly felicitous fiction were all part of the excellent working conditions he provides for his authors. Meanwhile, Terry McKiernan's gifts of skill and wit made the journey from manuscript to book painless, even when the manuscript literally lost its way.

Research grants from the Committee on Research and from the Social Sciences Division of the University of California at Santa Cruz enabled me to write this book expeditiously.

GWENDOLYN MINK

*Santa Cruz, California*

# Welfare as a Condition
# of Women's Equality

During the second decade of the twentieth century, progressive women activists invented welfare to provide mothers and their children a means to survive when breadwinning fathers either died or abandoned their families. During the 1930s, the local mothers' pension programs of the Progressive Era became part of the emerging national welfare state. The idea behind welfare was to relieve poor single mothers of the necessity of wage-earning so that they might engage in the full-time care of their children. Over the years, welfare came to be viewed less as an alternative to wages than as a safety net for mothers when wages were not available to them. Changes in the idea of welfare reflected changes in our assessments of mothers who are poor and single. Poor single mothers have always been judged by welfare policy, and developments in welfare policy have always either enhanced or undermined their rights, security, and ability to care for their children. Yet, beginning with Bill Clinton's famous 1992 campaign pledge to end welfare and throughout four years of debate about how to do it, hardly a soul worried about the impact of such a momentous change on poor single mothers as mothers and as citizens.

Some feminist activists labored to bring attention to how ending welfare would affect poor mothers' lives and rights. But among policy makers, even the usual champions of gender equality erased mothers from the debate. Most Democratic liberals in Congress who fought to save welfare did so for the sake of children, not mothers. They worried that ending the federal guarantee of economic assistance to poor families would plunge millions of children into poverty, making "cruelty to children an instrument of social policy."[1] But they cared little that new welfare provisions would pressure poor single mothers to surrender their civil rights as a condition of economic assistance. Much less did they care that rescinding the statutory entitlement to income security would punish poor single mothers for bearing and caring for children by compelling them to work outside the home.

Though Democrats balked at the most stringent Republican initiatives, such as a proposed three-month lifetime limit on food stamp eligibility for adults without dependents, the welfare debate revealed more grounds for consensus than for conflict. Both parties championed wage work and marriage as alternatives to welfare, promising to limit the period of welfare eligibility strictly, to penalize illegitimacy, and to require mothers to establish connections to men and the labor market. Both parties pegged their reforms not to the vast majority of recipients (75 percent) who use welfare for short periods, but to the minority (25 percent) of allegedly chronic recipients who need assistance for longer stretches of time. Both parties equated welfare use with welfare abuse, justifying increasingly punitive "reforms."

In the Senate, this bipartisan consensus produced an 87–12 vote to end the welfare guarantee and to encumber recipients with intrusive stipulations when welfare reform was first con-

sidered in 1995. Despite its Republican sponsorship and despite the Office of Management and Budget's prediction that
the measure would throw a million more children into poverty,
all but eleven Democratic senators supported the welfare bill.
During the 1996 debate in the House of Representatives,
Democrats demonstrated the strength of the bipartisan consensus when they offered a party proposal (the Castle-Tanner
substitute) that endorsed some of the most radical Republican
welfare principles. Recanting their 1995 pledge to defend the
welfare entitlement, House Democrats vowed to repeal it for
individuals and to replace it with block grants to states.[2] In
addition, the Democratic measure denied benefits to children
born to mothers receiving welfare and imposed paternity, child
support, and paternal visitation rules on all recipient mothers.

Notwithstanding the Democratic Party's long association
with civil rights and civil liberties, its alternative to Republican
welfare reform proposed policies that would invade poor
mothers' reproductive, conjugal, and family privacy rights.[3]
Moreover, notwithstanding the Democratic Party's feminist
sympathies, its alternative proposed to return poor single
mothers to patriarchal dependency on their children's biological fathers. One hundred fifty-nine House Democrats voted for
this baleful assault on the rights of poor mothers, including
Democrats who call themselves feminists: the Democratic co-
chair of the Congressional Women's Caucus (Nita Lowey,
D-New York), the former Democratic co-chair of the Caucus
(Patricia Schroeder, D-Colorado), the only woman in the Democratic leadership (Barbara Kennelly, D-Connecticut), twenty-
three of twenty-eight other Democratic women, and two past
presidents of the liberal Americans for Democratic Action
(Barney Frank, D-Massachusetts, and John Lewis, D-Georgia).
As one congressional feminist admitted of her colleagues,
when it comes to welfare "nobody cares about women."

With this vote, Democratic liberals and feminists banished

the welfare entitlement to history and abandoned welfare mothers to the Republicans' welfare police state. The Republican chair of the House Committee on Education and the Workforce gloated: "There is good news to announce on the floor of the House today. The good news basically is that all of those who have, over the last thirty some years, generated an unworkable welfare program, have now come to the floor and admitted that it does not work."[4] In the final hours of debate in both houses, the difference between Democrats and Republicans boiled down to whether states could use federal welfare money to provide vouchers for diapers and other government-approved goods to children whose families are removed from welfare after five years—hardly an issue of fundamental principle.[5] Democrats argued that children should not have to pay for their mothers' sins, that welfare reform should "be tough on parents, not tough on kids." As Senator John Breaux of Louisiana, author of the voucher amendment in the Senate, put it, "We should not be punishing the children for what the parents have not done correctly."[6] In contrast, Republicans fought to withhold palliatives for children they feared would undermine their message to mothers. But the two parties agreed that welfare reform should be tough on mothers and that the end of welfare should be the reform of poor women. President Clinton sealed the consensus when he signed the welfare bill—with vouchers—into law.

The broad support for disciplinary welfare reform is rooted in the view that mothers' poverty flows from moral failing. Both Democrats and Republicans emphasized the wrongs of mothers—their "unwillingness to work," their failure to marry (or stay married), their irresponsible sexuality and childbearing. Accordingly, the legislative debate about welfare was a contest among moral prescriptions, rather than a conflict between perspectives either on the role and responsibilities of

government or on the rights and responsibilities of women.
It was a genuine contest for a while. Democrats assigned priority to work-ethical stipulations backed by funding for child
care and job training; during the first round of debate in 1995,
Democrats accused Republicans of being "weak on work" and
called for more severe work requirements and time limits. Republicans, meanwhile, stressed marital family life backed by
work requirements and cold-turkey sanctions; they charged
Democrats with being soft on "family values" and fought
Democratic efforts to broaden hardship exceptions (as with
vouchers) to the new welfare rules. But these differences did
not subvert the bipartisan concordance against poor mothers'
rights and poor families' economic security.

About half the Senate Democrats and the majority of House
Democrats voted against the Republicans' Personal Responsibility and Work Opportunity Reconciliation Act (PRA) on final
passage. This partisan vote masks the strength and durability
of the bipartisan war against mothers who need welfare. The
PRA may have been Republican legislation, but the pledge to
end welfare was a Democratic president's inspiration. The PRA
may have been the crown jewel of the Republican pledge to
enact the Contract with America, but it was less a change in
policy than a culmination of thirty years of bipartisan efforts
to subdue poor mothers' welfare rights.

As we shall see, since 1967 both Democrats and Republicans
have insisted that fathers return at least to financial, if not marital, family headship. For mothers who decline association with
their children's fathers, both parties have prescribed work outside the home. Embracing the logic of welfare reform since
1967—and nationalizing many of the state-level reforms accomplished through presidential waiver[7] since 1988—the Personal Responsibility Act makes poor single mothers' decisions
for them, substituting moral prescription for economic mitiga-

tion of their poverty. Moreover, the Act withdraws rights from recipients, thereby restoring the moral regime that sifted, sorted, and ruled welfare applicants and recipients until the late 1960s.[8] Rights trampled by the welfare law include fundamental constitutional rights to make one's own decisions about marriage, about family life, and about procreation.[9] Also endangered is poor mothers' vocational freedom, that is, their Thirteenth Amendment freedom from coerced labor.[10]

Thirty years of welfare politics and welfare reform presaged many of the provisions of the Republicans' PRA, including the repeal of the welfare entitlement. The repeal of the welfare entitlement means that poor mothers have lost governmental assurance that their desperate economic circumstances will not deteriorate into abject destitution. Now they and their children no longer have a legally enforceable claim to benefits: in its statement of purposes, the PRA explicitly disclaims an entitlement for individuals. What's more, the new policy both invites and requires states to condition benefits not on need alone but also on moral conformity.

The change in welfare policy disables women's citizenship. Some feminists fought welfare reform for this reason. Calling attention to "welfare as a women's issue," we argued that "a war against poor women is a war against all women."[11] While this was a strategically useful rallying cry, it failed to rally many women, or feminists. The war against poor women was just that: a war specifically against poor women, and one in which many middle-class women participated on the anti-welfare side. Four of five Democratic women in the Senate voted *for* the PRA when it first came before the Senate in the summer of 1995. Only five of thirty-one Democratic women in the House opposed the Democratic welfare proposal that stripped poor mothers and children of an income security entitlement, coerced poor mothers into relations with biological fathers, and required single mothers to work both inside and outside the home. Across the country, a NOW–Legal Defense and Education Fund appeal for funds to support an economic justice litigator aroused so much hate mail that the organization stopped doing direct mail on the welfare issue.[12] A white and middle-class solipsism enforced a general feminist silence about the stakes of welfare provisions for poor women, and that silence gave permission to policymakers to treat punitive welfare reform as a no-lose situation. Welfare reform did not bear directly on the lives of most white, middle-class feminists, and so they did not mobilize their networks and raise their voices as they have in defending abortion rights or protesting domestic violence. When they did enter the debate, many middle-class feminists prescribed child support and wage work as alternatives to welfare. This echoed policymakers' claims that "real" welfare reform is to be found in the patriarchal family economy and in mothers' work outside the home.

Still, despite disagreements about welfare among women and feminists, there is some truth to the claim that welfare reform affects us all. Poor single mothers are most immediately and most brutally harmed by the Personal Responsibility Act, of course, but many of the law's incursions against their rights and protections potentially injure all women: for example, as Congress impairs the reproductive rights of poor women by paying states to reduce nonmarital births, it erodes the privileged constitutional status of reproductive rights as fundamental to all women's equality. Mandatory paternity establishment provisions likewise carry perils for all birth mothers, whether or not they are poor. Although the PRA requires disclosure of procreative relations from welfare mothers only, policymakers have proposed requiring mothers to identify biological fathers outside the welfare context: for example, President Clinton's 1994 welfare bill sought the establishment of paternity for *all* non-marital hospital births. Further, although poor single mothers are most directly endangered by the elimination of welfare's income entitlement, all mothers surrender equality in gender relations when government withdraws their safety net—their last-gasp means for economic independence from men. For these sorts of reasons, women's gender equality pivots on poor single mothers' rights, whether or not all women need to use those rights at any given time. Equality *among* women also pivots on poor single mothers' rights, for welfare law stratifies rights to the detriment of poor single mothers alone. Welfare law subverts women's equality not only by placing women's gender rights on a slippery downhill slope, but also by hardening hierarchies among women.

The subject of this book is the relationship between welfare rights and women's equality. I will examine the rights compromised or revoked by the PRA, considering how these losses burden poor single mothers' citizenship, and speculating whether the rights under challenge will prove strong enough to defend poor single mothers from the law's worst political effects. The PRA promises to end "welfare dependency" by returning mothers to economic relationships with fathers and, where those relationships fail, by speeding mothers into the labor market. I will argue that these prescriptions are ill-conceived and harmful, disabling poor single mothers' equality as citizens, as women and as mothers.

Poor single mothers' equality with men as well as with other women depends not on "making fathers pay" or on making mothers work, but on paying for the work mothers *do*—as caregivers for their children. Without social provision for caregiving, all mothers who work inside the home are deprived of equal citizenship, for they alone are not paid for their labor. Without earnings, women who work full- or part-time as their children's care-givers are ideologically unequal in a political culture that prizes income-producing work as the currency of virtue. They are also unequal at law: worth less when juries assess economic damages to them in tort claims, and worth less to juries awarding civil damages in wrongful death claims.[13] Moreover, care-giving mothers do not have marital freedom: lacking the means to exit marriages, they lack the freedom to choose to stay in them. Mothers who do dare to exit or avoid marriage do not enjoy vocational liberty: unpaid for their work in the home, single mothers are forced either by law or by economic circumstance to choose wages over children.

## Welfare and Citizenship

Citizenship is the web of relationships between the individual and the state, relationships that incur both rights and obligations. In our constitutional democracy, the basic rights of citizenship are political. Citizenship confers such political rights as suffrage and such obligations as jury duty. These rights and obligations are not directly reciprocal: the right to vote does not oblige us to do so, for example, any more than the obligation to jury duty gives us the right to be selected to serve. Our strongest obligations are enforced by law: accordingly, men's duty to contribute to the national defense has been enforced by military conscription. But many of our obligations are wholly ethical: we enter into public service or participate in community life because we are supposed to, not because we are required to. Perhaps the most coherent enumeration of the ethical and legal obligations of citizenship is contained in the oath of naturalization—with which only immigrant citizens ever become familiar.

If some of our obligations are codified in scattered statutes and others are simply implied by the political culture, our rights are explicitly enumerated in the Constitution or have been definitively located in its penumbras by the Supreme Court. We enjoy most political rights not because we earned them or because they are our moral due, but because a democratic political community bestows political rights on citizens as a condition of its own existence. In theory, political rights are universal: we do not each have to prove we deserve the right to vote or to speak or to be fairly tried. Because political rights are universal, we are theoretically equal as citizens.

Not all individuals have always been considered citizens, however. Under slave law, African Americans were chattel rather than persons; with the *Dred Scott* decision, African Americans, both enslaved and free, were declared ineligible for citizenship.[14] According to the naturalization law of 1790, only whites could become naturalized citizens. A change in the law in 1870 admitted Africans to naturalization, but Asian immigrants remained barred from naturalization—and hence from citizenship—until 1952. For the native-born and naturalized, restrictions on citizenship were relaxed, in theory, when the Fifteenth Amendment conferred political rights on male citizens of all races in 1870. However, political practice withheld political rights from most African Americans and many Mexican Americans until the 1960s. Meanwhile, the Supreme Court explained in 1875 that women were not citizens in any sense that implied rights of political participation.[15] Although women won the right to participate in elections in 1920, they were denied collateral rights and obligations of citizenship (for example, jury duty) well into the 1970s and continue to be excluded from certain citizenship obligations even at the twentieth century's end (for example, draft registration and Army combat duty). As a result of these varied exclusions from and distinctions within citizenship, full citizenship has been categorical rather than universal throughout most of U. S. history, with rights inhering in the racial, cultural, and gender status of individuals rather than in the individual as such.

Many rights that we ordinarily refer to as civil rights and liberties flow from the formal procedural and participatory guarantees of citizenship. Since the 1930s, rights that most directly affect the integrity of democratic processes have received special recognition and protection, most notably the rights to speak, associate, and assemble.[16] Also in the 1930s, the Supreme Court began to question the categorical distribution of rights, such as the right to counsel and the right to own property.[17] By the 1950s, the Court had declared "that the constitution of the United States . . . forbids, so far as civil and political rights are concerned, discrimination by the general government."[18] This assertion opened the way to the review and revision of legislation that created distinctions among individuals, particularly distinctions that disabled claims to full citizenship. Among the civil rights receiving heightened judicial protection were the right to marry (or not to) and the right to procreate (or not to).[19]

Beginning in the 1960s, certain rights deemed fundamental to democratic life became available to everyone: the right to counsel (1963); voting rights (1965); the right to be tried by a jury of one's peers (1976). But this universalizing of political rights did not guarantee citizen equality. To universalize rights is to vest everyone with the same rights, to erase categorical distinctions. Even as political distinctions disappear, however, social inequalities differentiate citizen capacities to exercise rights. A homeless person has no address and cannot register to vote; a hungry person may not have the time to devote to her own political education; an illiterate person cannot read her ballot and therefore cannot cast it. Because homelessness, hunger, illiteracy, and other social conditions encroach on political rights, most serious democracies have recognized that the transition from categorical to universal citizenship requires mitigating social inequality. Policies that allay unequal social conditions include provisions guaranteeing the basic economic security of citizens. These provisions comprise social rights—primordial claims to those social supports that enable one to live and to participate in the political community. The United States has not offered generous social supports to its citizens, but it has provided for minimal subsistence (a safety net) to cushion different categories of need.

Most political rights are grounded in the Constitution and only with great difficulty can be denied. The Supreme Court occasionally has insisted, moreover, that certain constitutional guarantees must be secured through social provision: in *Gideon v. Wainwright,* for example, the Court ordered government to furnish indigent criminal defendants with counsel, arguing that the fundamental right to counsel was meaningless for defendants who could not afford to pay for an attorney.[20] Most social rights, however, derive not from the Constitution but from claims endorsed by political majorities through the legislative process. Though they cannot be denied so long as majorities support them, social rights are hostage to shifting political winds. In U. S. policy parlance we call legislated social rights "entitlements" and situate them along a continuum of claims running from privileges to constitutional guarantees.[21]

Although social rights are weaker than political rights, the full and universal exercise of political rights pivots on their availability. Like political rights, social rights are conceptually universal as they guarantee everyone their right to a subsistence sufficient to ensure survival and to facilitate independent participation in the life of the community. But where political rights *assume* equality among the individuals who possess them, social rights *enable* equality by countervailing inequalities among individuals. Because inequalities are various, most social rights become targeted entitlements in practice. We may all have the same right to vote regardless of social station, but we are entitled to different social benefits depending on what our needs are and what our contributions have been. The elderly receive retirement benefits, for example, while the sick poor receive Medicaid and laid-off workers receive unemployment insurance. Thus entitlements are categorical, but have the effect of universalizing the political rights of citizenship.

The specific content of most social entitlements varies with the needs and circumstances of individuals, and so the strength of specific entitlements often depends on what we think of the people claiming them. The strongest entitlements—those most difficult to deny—are those we link to sweat and to sacrifice. The veteran, for example, is said to deserve his GI benefits because military service entails risks to life and limb. The worker is said to have earned his old-age pension through paid employment and taxes. The concept of earned benefits rests on the fiction that individuals get back from the benefits system only what they paid in, and no more. But even the most popular social benefits are structured to provide in part according to need and so are not strictly tied to the beneficiary's degree of contribution.[22] For example, the average social security beneficiary who retired at age sixty-five in 1995 would get back all the taxes she contributed to the social security system within three and a half years.[23] Although "earned" social security benefits eventually become "welfare" for retired workers, we do not begrudge the elderly their pensions. Rather, we believe that retired workers have paid for their benefits at least metaphorically, through lifelong attachment to the labor market.

The idea that certain benefits are earned appeals to the ethic of contract, expressing the view that government owes the individual his benefit in exchange for services rendered. If recipients of putatively contractual benefits are the first among citizens of the welfare state, the most vulnerable and unequal citizens have been those who need their benefits and who receive them as a gratuity from government rather than as their due. Income support for needy citizens tends to be stingier and more begrudging than for citizens who are believed to have paid for it.[24] Hence, for example, even though mothers in the survivors' insurance system and mothers in the welfare system are all mothers parenting alone, a widowed mother whose husband paid social security taxes receives a survivors' stipend for herself and her children four times greater than the average monthly welfare grant received by divorced or never-married mothers and their children.[25]

Both discursively and structurally, welfare—economic assistance to poor single mothers and their children—affirmed rather than repaired inequality. During the 1960s and early 1970s, the national welfare rights movement fought to secure rights for welfare participants—the right to move to another state, for example, as well as the right to a fair hearing. Welfare rights litigation made headway beginning in 1968: following the Supreme Court's announcement in *King v. Smith* that state welfare rules must conform to the national statutory purpose of welfare, a single set of national criteria determined poor families' eligibility.[26] And following the Supreme Court's decision in *Shapiro v. Thompson* that welfare residency requirements compromised poor families' "basic right" to travel, mothers who received welfare were afforded certain constitutional protections.[27] In these respects, rights of national citizenship were extended to poor single mothers. Yet even during this period of widening rights within welfare, racism, sexism, and moral stigma poisoned poor single mothers' right *to* welfare. Moreover, the structure of welfare distinguished poor single mothers from other recipients of social entitlements. While payment levels for widowed mothers and their children in the survivors' insurance system are nationally determined and uniform, for example, welfare benefit levels have been controlled by the states. Hence, even before the Personal Responsibility Act, the degree of support available to a mother and her children depended on where they resided: for example, 1995 cash payments in Mississippi were $120 per month for a family of three, while in Connecticut they were more than $600.[28]

Historically, benefits for those who most need them have been most fragile—most susceptible to political attack. This is why, despite their posturing against the welfare state as a whole, the Republicans in the 104th Congress singled out economic assistance for poor single mothers and their children for repeal. Calling recipients "lazy" and their children "illegitimate," welfare reformers played to the view that welfare lies outside the social contract. Ridiculing welfare as a payment to women who do not work, they made the welfare entitlement very easy to deny.

In rejecting poor single mothers' social claim to economic assistance, welfare reformers did not end welfare absolutely but rather restricted its availability through time limits and rules for participation. Many of the rules for participation are burdens that government cannot impose on citizens directly: for example, government cannot pressure a woman directly to choose abortion any more than it can pressure her directly to choose childbirth.[29] Nor can government force an individual into a particular job—except through military conscription—especially if that job is unpaid.

Since one mission of the Personal Responsibility Act is precisely to pressure women's rights by regulating how poor mothers exercise them, it may not withstand constitutional scrutiny.[30] From the standpoint of liberty that would be good news. However, in the absence of a recognized right to welfare, constitutionally suspicious welfare policy may be succeeded by no welfare policy at all. This would be devastating for equal citizenship. So it is important to connect the recovery of poor mothers' rights *within* welfare to their right *to receive* welfare in the first place.

To some extent we can derive a right to welfare through constitutional reasoning: as I will argue later, a socially provided income guarantee is (or ought to be) a condition of reproductive, marital, family, and vocational rights, as well as a matter of equal protection. Ultimately, however, the claim to a welfare right is a political one, for we lack a strong jurisprudential tradition binding economic provision to constitutional guarantees: the Court generally does not require government to subsidize the exercise of a right (say, reproductive choice) even though without a subsidy (Medicaid funding) a person may not be able to exercise her right (for example, choose abortion).[31] In fact, the Court emphatically rejects the claim that government bears affirmative obligations to support fundamental rights, arguing that "'the Due Process Clauses . . . confer no affirmative right to governmental aid, even where such aid may be necessary to secure life, liberty, or property interests of which the government itself may not deprive the individual.'"[32] Nor does the Court hold government constitutionally responsible to provide for the economic security of its citizens.

Notwithstanding these judicial restraints on what it compels, however, the Constitution does permit us to imagine different ways to enforce its meaning legislatively: the Fourteenth Amendment gives Congress the responsibility to enact laws that enforce its provisions, including its clause promising "equal protection of the law."[33] More to the point, the Constitution permits us to defend rights with remedies, including social supports without which the rights of some citizens would either erode or disappear.

The equality clause of the Fourteenth Amendment is the

wellspring of doctrine and policy universalizing citizenship. Beginning in the 1970s, the Supreme Court brought women within equality's purview, deriving from the promise of equal treatment the basic civil rights of women. The Court has generally declined to require equal treatment where women are differently positioned than men: for example, in a decision that still stands, the Court in 1974 ruled that discrimination against pregnant women workers is not discrimination based on gender, and thus not prohibited by the equal protection clause (*Geduldig v. Aiello* 417 U.S. 484). Similarly, in 1981 the Court upheld a statutory rape law under which only girls could be victims (*Michael M. v. Superior Court of Sonoma County* 450 U.S. 464). Such exceptions to equal treatment often have impaired women's equality.

However, the Court also has occasionally noticed that equality may sometimes require treating women and men differently by vesting women with rights or benefits that are uniquely their own. Thus Justice O'Connor argued after reconsidering *Roe v. Wade* that "the liberty of the woman is at stake in a sense unique to the human condition and so unique to the law. . . . The destiny of the woman must be shaped to a large extent on her own conception of her spiritual imperatives and her place in society."[34] The Court has likewise acknowledged that at the conjuncture of biology and gender may reside inequalities that only remedies gauged to women's circumstances can repair.[35] For example, in a Title VII decision upholding California's job security guarantee for women workers who take pregnancy leave, the Court noted that the goal of the gender-specific disability protection "is to guarantee women the basic right to participate fully and equally in the workforce, without denying them the fundamental right to full participation in family life."[36] Drawing a distinction between gender-sensitive enabling rights and gender-prescriptive restrictions, the Court also has cautioned: "But such classifications may not be used, as they once were . . . to create or perpetuate the legal, social, and economic inferiority of women."[37]

Gendered rights are tricky business, as the differential treatment of women in law and policy has too often meant our unequal treatment. Moreover, policies or rights derived for the generic woman risk defining the experiences and needs of particular groups of women as the experiences and needs of all. They further risk prescribing or ascribing roles and choices to women who may rather eschew them. That said, I think too many inequalities flow from ignoring women's various gender-based needs and dilemmas. These inequalities find an excuse in difference, handicap women in private and public relations with men, and command conformity to white male rules as the price of women's civic and social incorporation.

But we don't need to claim rights for women only. We can draw from women's diverse gendered experiences to design policies that correct inequalities attached to those experiences. We can write such gender-sensitive laws in gender-neutral language—as parental leave policy is written, for example, and as welfare policy was from 1935 to 1996. We can consciously avoid assuming or requiring that *all* women conform to a single gender role, and avoid obligating *only* women to perform that role. But we cannot cure inequality where it is most gendered—in sexual, reproductive, and family relations—without addressing the ways in which that inequality directly and disproportionately burdens women.

One such inequality is the economic disfranchisement of mothers who are their children's care-givers. Mothers who work inside the home raising children are deprived of fair remuneration for their labor, and thus of the means for independence, because we do not impute economic value to the work they do. In marriages, mothers who work inside the home surrender their economic personhood to husbands and occupy the legal status of dependent. Their lack of independent economic resources—earnings—skews power relations in the family: some mothers may feel tethered to husbands because they could not survive the economic consequences of leaving them. Single mothers bear the costs of economic disfranchisement most acutely, for they must accept destitution as a condition of caring for their children. Unpaid and disdained, they are expected to forswear child-raising for full-time wage-earning. Mothers who work inside the home caring for children, then, are disproportionately dependent on men if married and disproportionately poor, if not. These private inequalities have public effects, foreclosing such mothers' independent citizenship.

We should not think of welfare as a subsidy for dependence; nor should we think of it as an income substitute for the wage earned by breadwinners—fathers—in the labor market. Rather, we should reconceive welfare as the income *owed* to persons who work inside the home caring for, nurturing, and protecting children. As it has been for sixty years, welfare should be available to solo care-giving parents of either sex. But though sex-blind, welfare cannot be gender-neutral, for it should assign economic value to a role mostly performed by women: care-giving. Thus conceived, welfare would enhance equality by compensating solo care-giving mothers for the work they do and extending to them the work-based social rights of citizenship.

As a social right, welfare must remedy material as well as gender conditions that impede equality—that stratify citizenship. Accordingly, while welfare should establish the principle that all family care-giving is work, it should support that work in a way that redistributes income security toward the most vulnerable family care-givers. Mothers who need to leave marriages or who are already single and poor are most at risk of exploitation and destitution because they must both care and provide for their children. Welfare should redress this inequality, thereby guarding the rights and promoting the independence of mothers who must parent alone. Meanwhile, the availability of welfare for single care-givers would enhance equality in marriage: giving married mothers the means to exit marriages, welfare would give them a choice to remain, as well.

As an income for poor single care-givers and as a safety net for all care-givers who might find themselves alone and poor, welfare is a prerequisite for equality in the family, in the labor market, and in the state. As such, welfare should be a right, not a gratuity—a claim backed by law and courts that should be irresistible, or at least very hard to deny. We can locate a welfare right in the penumbras of other rights. In one sense, it is a right upon which other rights, such as reproductive choice, depend. But welfare is also a right unto itself: under the Thirteenth and Fourteenth Amendments, everyone has the right to be paid for their labor.

## Racism, White Feminism, and Mothers' Work

Recent history demonstrates some of the links between welfare and women's equality. Although welfare has hardly liberated women from poverty, for thirty years it has emancipated mothers from utter dependency on a male income and from gross exploitation in low-wage jobs, and it has allowed them to care for their children. During the late 1960s, the Supreme Court confirmed that welfare was a statutory right and applied constitutional principles to its administration. This meant that all who fit the eligibility criteria established in welfare law could expect to receive benefits. Since welfare promised assistance to adult care-givers and their children based on economic need, it became a security policy for mothers on the threshold of poverty.

The availability of welfare enabled poor mothers and those at risk of poverty to make choices about their lives even when those choices meant losing labor market wages—either their own or their husbands'. This entitlement was especially important for mothers who earned low wages outside the home or no wages at all for their work inside the home. Welfare made it possible for such mothers to exit sexually hostile work environments, abusive relationships, and unhappy marriages.[38] It permitted poor women to make their own reproductive and parenting decisions. It afforded poor single mothers the means to navigate for themselves between the dual responsibilities of care-giving and providing. Because it enabled mothers to act upon their relational choices and responsibilities, welfare fostered not dependency but independence.

Such a claim may strike many as counterintuitive. Most people understand welfare as a "hand out" and argue that one cannot be handed independence but must achieve it. This view girds a restrictive work-ethical perspective on social rights in the United States, one that caps possibilities for redistributive social policies and that underlies numerous gender-based inequities in the welfare state. But we need not abjure the work ethic to make a case for welfare. Quite the opposite: the work ethic ought to give legitimacy to welfare, for the care-giving performed mostly by mothers is *work*.

The early twentieth-century initiators of welfare policy understood this and wondered how poor mothers who were parenting alone could be expected to perform two jobs. As a solution to the double burden, welfare innovators designed pensions for single mothers so they could work in the home raising their children. The pensions were highly contingent, however. Conflating poor mothers' economic needs with their cultural and moral practices, welfare innovators encumbered pensions with troubling rules that conditioned economic assistance on cultural and moral remediation. Early twentieth-century welfare policy thus prescribed inequality rather than equality, social intervention rather than social rights, leaving legacies of cultural and racial hierarchy among women and of gender-based inequity in the welfare state.[39]

The best of early welfare policy—social recognition for mothers' care-giving work—has disappeared from welfare policy and discourse. What has carried over from the earlier period is the idea that welfare policy should supply moral and cultural guidance to poor single mothers, should be "tough on moms" for the sake of their kids. Policy-makers have negated the mother-work of poor women partly because of *who* they imagine welfare mothers to be. Listen to President Clinton explain his decision to repeal sixty years of social policy: "The poverty population of America was fundamentally different than it is now. . . . When welfare was created the typical welfare recipient was a miner's widow with no education, small children, husband dies in the mine, no expectation that there was a job for the widow to do or that she ever could do it, very few out-of-wedlock pregnancies and births. The whole dynamics were different then."[40] What can he have meant? That if the welfare population were still 89 percent white and 61 percent widowed, as it was in 1939, welfare would not need to be reformed?

With President Clinton, most Democrats and Republicans imagine welfare mothers to be reckless breeders who bear children to avoid work.[41] Such vintage stereotypes have bipartisan roots, and were popularized beginning in the 1960s by Republican Richard Nixon, southern Democrat Russell Long, and sometime Democrat George Wallace. Even Lyndon Johnson, often credited for expanding welfare as part of his War on

Poverty, shared these views: he called for limits on payments to non-marital children and complained that their mothers "sit around and breed instead of going out to work."[42]

Into the 1990s, the racial mythology of welfare cast the welfare mother as Black, pinned the need for reform on her character, and at least implicitly defined Black women as other people's workers rather than their own families' mothers.[43] Racially charged images of lazy, promiscuous, and matriarchal women have dominated welfare discourse for quite some time, inflaming demands that mothers who need welfare—though *perhaps* not their children—must pay for their improvident behavior through work, marriage, or destitution.[44]

Welfare reformers in both parties have maintained that poor single mothers must pay for their deviant personal morality and family practices by earning wages. Almost all policymakers and most commentators chorus the mantra "work, not welfare," even those who believe that "the best place for mothers" is in the home. Many welfare reformers view work requirements as necessary not because all mothers should be in the labor market, but because *poor single* mothers ought to be. Some reformers argue that outside work will improve these women's private morality: "tough work requirements [may] cause young women to delay pregnancy until marriage."[45] Others offer outside work as punishment for single mothers' manifestly depraved morality: defending the Republicans' refusal to fund child care adequately, conservative James Talent (R-Missouri) told the House of Representatives, "If you restore the two parent family, then you don't *need* child care."[46] Both comments prove that it is not work, but marriage—not sweat, but a ceremony—that many reformers view as the real alternative to welfare.

If racism has permitted policymakers to negate poor single mothers as citizens and mothers, white middle-class feminism has provided those policymakers with an excuse. White middle-class feminists' emphasis on women's right to work outside the home—accompanied by women's increased presence in the labor force—gave cover to conservatives eager to require wage work of single mothers even as they championed the traditional family.

Most of the policy claims made by second-wave feminists have emphasized women's right to participate in white men's world and have made work outside the home a defining element of women's full and equal citizenship. White middle-class feminists have responded to their particular historical experiences, experiences drawn by an ethos of domesticity which had confined them to the home. As they entered the labor market, these women did not spurn family work; rather, they found their energy doubly taxed by the dual responsibility of earning and caring. Accordingly, many feminists called for labor market policies addressing the family needs that fall disproportionately on women—parental leave and child care policies, for example. Their concern has been to ease the contradictions between wage work and family life. Their focus has been how family needs impede opportunities and achievements in the labor market; their goals have been labor policies that relieve women's family responsibilities (such as child care) and strengthen women's rights in the workplace (such as wage equity). They have not been so interested in winning social policies to support women where we meet our family responsibilities: in the home. In the absence of feminist affirmation of the child-raising and home management work mothers do, poor mothers' right to provide care for their own children has been only faintly defended.

Although white middle-class feminists have been reluctant to make equality claims for women as family workers, certainly they have never denied that women's family care-giving work has social value. During the early 1970s, for example, some feminists called for a recalculation of the gross national product to include the economic value of women's work in the home.[47] Many radical and socialist feminists challenged the sexual division of labor, illuminating connections between women's unpaid labor in the home and their gender-based inequality. Some on the feminist left drew the conclusion that "women's work" should be remunerated—that women should be paid "wages for housework."[48] But most white middle-class feminists— liberal, radical, and socialist—found the home to be the prime site of women's oppression and accordingly stressed the liberating potential of participation in the labor market.

The popular feminist claim that women earn independence, autonomy, and equality through wages long has divided feminists along class and race lines, as women of color and poor white women have not usually discovered equality in sweated labor. On the contrary: especially for women of color, wage work has been a mark of inequality: expected by the white society for whom they work; necessary because their male kin cannot find jobs or cannot earn family-supporting wages; and exploitative because their earnings keep them poor. Thus the rights to have and care for their own children—to work inside the home—have been touchstone goals of their struggles for equality. The fact that different women are differently positioned in the nexus among care-giving, wage-earning, and inequality separated feminists from one another on the welfare issue, and separated them as well from mothers who need welfare. One measure of welfare politics among women was the small scale of feminist activism for welfare justice— especially by comparison to vigils against O.J. Simpson, or lobbying against the late-term abortion bill or boycotts against *The People vs. Larry Flynt*.

Dominating feminist contributions to the welfare debate were fears that any formal recognition for mothers' economic

needs as family workers might reinstitutionalize separate, gendered spheres. Also prominent was the view that wage work is
"good" for women, yielding them an income, adult company,
and incentive to delay childbirth.[49] In the main, white middle-
class feminists assumed that poor women should exercise their
rights not as they themselves choose but as white middle-class
feminists choose. According to this view, women ought to
choose fertility control rather than childbirth if they are poor;
ought to choose child care provided by others over raising their
own children; ought to choose gainful employment over
domesticity. These feminist logics helped forestall a defense
against the bipartisan assault on poor mothers' citizenship.

Out of the feminist emphasis on winning rights in the workplace has emerged, sotto voce, an expectation that women
ought to work outside the home and an assumption that *any* job
outside the home, including caring for other people's children,
is more socially productive than caring for one's own.[50] Feminists in Congress betrayed this bias, voting unfazed to require
poor single mothers to work outside the home both as a condition of receiving welfare and as a consequence of time limits.
Few seemed terribly concerned about the availability of jobs at
living wages for poor single mothers: they voted to compel
wage work even against evidence that most poor single mothers who work outside the home thirty to forty hours per week
live below the poverty line.[51]

Although feminism is fundamentally about winning women
choices, our labor market bias has put much of feminism not on
the side of vocational choice—the choice to work inside or
outside the home—but on the side of wage-earning for all
women. Thus most congressional feminists, along with many
feminists across the country, have conflated their own *right* to
work outside the home with poor single mothers' *obligation*
to do so. This is an obligation of no small significance for poor
single mothers, who are conscripted into wage work under the

new welfare law. Its work provisions uncontested during two years of legislative debate, the Personal Responsibility Act transforms outside work from an ethical obligation to a legal one. Work requirements and time limits supported by both Democrats and Republicans, feminists and patriarchalists, give mothers who need welfare no choice but to work outside the home. Such coerced labor, backed up by legal sanction for mothers receiving welfare and by threat of physical endangerment for mothers who have exhausted their eligibility, meets the Supreme Court's definition of involuntary servitude, prohibited by the Thirteenth Amendment.[52]

The labor market focus of second-wave feminism has accomplished much for women—most importantly establishing equality claims for women as wage earners. Contemporary feminist calls for further labor market reforms—such as an increased minimum wage, gender-sensitive unemployment insurance, comparable worth, and child care—rightly point out the persisting impediments to women's equality as labor market citizens. The problem is not with the specific content of feminist agendas but with their general one-sidedness. While women's inequality in the labor market has a lot to do with poor single mothers' need for welfare, so, too, does the inequality to which those mothers are consigned because they are doing the work of two parents on less than half the income of two-parent families and with only half the time.

## Enabling Equality

Most single mothers work outside the home, and most single mothers who receive welfare want to. The question raised by welfare law is whether social policy should dictate that they *must?* Poor single mothers already shoulder a double burden in parenting; should social policy require them to perform yet another job? The issue is not whether women with care-giving responsibilities should enjoy full opportunity and equality in the labor market. Of course they should. The issue is coercion. Why should poor single mothers—and *only* poor single mothers—be forced by law to work outside the home?

Care-giving, especially of young children—and 63 percent of mothers on welfare have children under age five—involves more than baby-sitting. It includes managing a household, doing housework, and, most important, nurturing, loving, and comforting. Meeting the basic challenges of family work— shopping for bargains on a tight budget, preparing edible and nutritious meals with very little money, schlepping to the laundromat without a car, attending to a child's schedule of needs, cleaning, mending, caring—takes time, effort, energy, and responsibility (the very skills and sacrifices assigned economic value in the outside labor market). For a solo care-giver who is poor, it can be a labor-intensive, full-time job.

Except for a few young men in my classes who insist that mothering is simply love, I think most people understand that the care-giving mostly provided by mothers is actually work. Disagreements arise over whether that work is worth anything if it is performed for one's own family. One problem is that patriarchal tradition, at least under capitalism, assigned wages to men who in turn paid for their families. This closeted mothers' care-giving in the private sphere and concealed its independent economic value. Another problem is that whether we impute any value to family work depends on *whose* family we're talking about.

Republicans and Democrats occasionally have acknowledged that mothers' care-giving work has value; symbolically, at least, they have even remunerated it. But the value they have assigned to mothers' work inside the home has depended on the class and color of the mother. The very week it *negated* the care-giving work performed by poor single mothers for their own children by giving final approval to the Personal Responsibility Act, Congress *affirmed* the care-giving work of middle-class homemakers by granting them rights to their own Independent Retirement Accounts (IRAs).[53] According to Representative Nancy Johnson (R-Connecticut), the measure "dramatically helps women. For the first time it puts in the law the legislation we need to give women who stay at home and take care of the children the same IRA rights as anyone else in America. This is a sea change. This is good legislation. This is about equality for all of us. This is about building a strong future for the families of our Nation."[54] Not only did enactment of this provision deepen existing differentiations in law between married and unmarried mothers, between white women and women of color, and between rich women and poor, it also formalized a distinction between poor single mothers' worthless *time* in the home and married, middle-class mothers' worthy *work* there. IRAs, after all, are an untaxed portion of *earned* income.

Clearly, legislators do understand that what some domestic mothers do is not pass the time, but *work*. One challenge, then, is to win recognition that *all* mothers' care-giving is work. Another is to indemnify that work with a socially provided income. Remuneration for mothers' care-giving work ought not to be too difficult to calculate, for much of the work done by mothers already has a market price if performed for someone else's family. We pay teachers, for example, as well as psychologists, nurses, accountants, chauffeurs, launderers, child-care workers, housecleaners, cooks, waitresses, and even personal shoppers. The Personal Responsibility Act itself conceives of care-giving as work, for it permits recipients to work off their benefits by caring for other recipients' children.[55]

That Republicans and Democrats could vote one day to compel maternal employment and vote two days later to reward maternal domesticity follows from the worry that not all mothers do their care-giving jobs equally well. I've heard feminists and patriarchalists alike argue that "those people" are bad mothers who ought not to bear and raise children at all; that people should have children only if they can afford them; that motherhood is a choice, not a necessity. From this point of view, social provision for care-giving is a moral hazard, encouraging procreative irresponsibility and subsidizing lousy mothers.

This assessment suggests that if only poor women would control their fertility there would be no need for welfare. Hence welfare reformers have favored proposals to condition welfare on the use of Norplant, to disqualify children from benefits if they are born to mothers on welfare, to offer incentive payments to states to lower their non-marital birth rates, and to restrict care-giving by unmarried teenage mothers. For poor women who continue to bear children despite disincentives to do so, welfare reformers condition the right to care for children on poor mothers' return to the patriarchal family. Hence, welfare law now requires poor mothers to identify biological fathers, associate with them, and thereby supply them with claims to parental rights.[56] And hence, welfare law now forbids mothers who remain single to work inside the home caring for their own children.[57] These various measures offend the procreative and family liberties that inhere in equal citizenship.

Constitutional doctrine holds that procreative liberty includes the right to choose motherhood, not just the right to avoid it.[58] Family liberty includes a constitutionally protected right to the "care, custody, management and companionship" of one's own children, a right "far more precious . . . than property rights."[59] The Court reaffirmed this right even after enactment of the Personal Responsibility Act placed poor mothers' parental rights in jeopardy.[60] The right to parent is a strong right, one that compels "a momentum for respect lacking when appeal is made to liberties which derive merely from shifting economic arrangements."[61] Family liberty reinforces procreative liberty, guaranteeing to all women who choose to become mothers the right to "direct the upbringing and education of children under their control."[62] Notably, both reproductive and family rights are conferred on individuals, not on procreative units or on particular family forms.

Reproductive and family rights provide strong defenses against eugenic and moral policing of care-giving mothers, but only if such rights are universal. If enforced for all care-giving mothers, they provide a shield against all but the most compellingly justified intrusions by government—where children have been abused or abandoned, for example—and thus against the welfare police state erected by the PRA. If enforced for all women with reproductive decisions to make, these rights enlarge choice by permitting even poor women to become mothers. However, for all women to enjoy them, repoductive and family rights require supplemental, enabling rights—to services that permit women to choose not to become mothers (such as Medicaid abortions) and to social provision that guarantees basic economic security to women who choose to do so (such as welfare). Just as the right to counsel would have no meaning in the absence of legal services for defendants, reproductive and family rights cease to be universal rights in the absence of social supports for the range of reproductive and family decisions women must make.

As remuneration for real work and as a dimension of reproductive and family rights, social support for poor single mothers' care-giving work would correct the unequal distribution of rights among women and would safeguard all mothers' independence in relations with men. In turn, reproductive and family rights would defend poor mothers against eugenic and moral policing of their care-giving work. This nexus among income security and reproductive and family liberties strengthens the right to welfare. To be sure, linking childbearing and child-rearing rights—to one another and to welfare—is fraught with risks, especially of essentializing women as mothers and of returning us to a separate sphere of citizenship. Still, ignoring the interdependence of personal liberties and economic security undermines the rights of women who are most vulnerable to inequality. What's more, ignoring the work women do in the very roles associated with our inequality punishes women for meeting their gender assignment.

Unless we can establish a right to welfare—a right to social provision for poor single mothers—inequality will persist where it is most gendered, in sexual, reproductive, and family relations. A right to income support in return for poor single mothers' care-giving work would redistribute choice and power on the neglected side of the gender divide, where mothers' care-giving work currently earns them only legal and economic dependency on men. But although a care-giver's income would address the gender divide, it need not reproduce that divide. Rights that accommodate mothers' care-giving work need not ascribe that work to all women, nor *only* to women: men can mother, too. Nor should such rights undermine women's choices and equality claims in the labor market. Rather, they should widen options by respecting differences among citizens. Waged workers and unwaged workers, women and men, poor and rich, single and married, parents and childless—are not fungible citizens. This is why social rights such as welfare are a condition of equal citizenship.

# 2

## How We Got Welfare Reform

### A Legislative History

For thirty years, politicians and voters have traded ugly tales about poor single mothers who need welfare. Seventy-two percent of mothers receiving welfare have no more than two children, and 61 percent of recipient mothers do not bear children while on welfare.[1] Yet everybody seems to know someone who has had extra babies to get more welfare. Most adult recipients would like to be in the labor market: 39 percent combined wages with welfare or cycled between them; the majority of recipients leave welfare within two years; and two-thirds of mothers who leave welfare do so to take jobs.[2] But everybody seems to know someone who refused work because she enjoyed "welfare as a way of life." There is no evidence that welfare causes poor unmarried mothers to be mothers, to be unmarried, or to be poor; and the average monthly welfare benefit ($377 for a family of four in 1995) hardly supports a desirable standard of living for mothers who parent alone. Yet everybody seems to know someone who didn't marry so she could milk the public treasury for welfare benefits. Only 1.2 percent of welfare mothers have been under age eighteen at the time they received benefits; teenagers account for a smaller proportion of non-marital births today than twenty years ago; and more than half of non-marital children are born to mothers aged twenty to twenty-nine.[3] But everyone seems to know "babies having babies" who are subsidized by welfare. Mythical welfare mothers have powered welfare politics for as long as I can remember and have kept welfare reform high on the national agenda.

Democratic Congresses and Republican presidents successfully amended welfare policy six times between 1967 and 1988, each time fanning public hostility toward mothers who are single and poor with promises to constrain their choices and reform their behaviors. Despite differences of emphasis, each policy change—in 1967, 1971, 1974, 1981, 1984, and 1988— moved incrementally in a singular direction, attaching national moral conditions to welfare benefits and backing them up with work requirements.

The following discussion will explore the persistence of moralism in welfare policy, from welfare's origins through the half-dozen rounds of reform to its recent repeal. I will first summarize the main elements of welfare reform, highlighting some of the ideological continuities between older efforts to fix welfare and the recent decision to end it. Next, I will sketch the history of welfare in this century, showing that the moralism that has so excited welfare politics over the past thirty years has always been at the core of welfare policy. I will then discuss how Supreme Court decisions during the late 1960s and early 1970s imperiled welfare's moralism with welfare rights. When the Court linked rights to welfare, recipients won their claim to national citizenship protections. Correspondingly, states lost prerogative to treat equally needy poor mothers differently based on moral distinctions among them. Defending moralism, though at the expense of states' rights, Congress swiftly moved to nationalize "the carrot and the stick"[4] through explicit moral stipulations and economic sanctions in the federal welfare law. Thus commenced the legislative juggernaut that would first sever rights from welfare, then end welfare's guarantee of income security for single mothers and their children.

## A Brief Review of Welfare Reform

Across the decades, a principal aim of welfare fixers has been to restore the system's moral levers. A recurrent theme in legislative debates has been how to induce poor single mothers to conform to patriarchal conventions: how to oblige them to bear and raise children in marriages; and, failing that, how to return mothers who parent independently of men to social and financial dependency on them. Despite their broadsides against "dependency" welfare reformers have been less concerned that poor single mothers are economically dependent than that they have been dependent on government. They expect that mothers will be dependent, but insist that they be dependent on men. Indeed, since the 1940s, reformers have been troubled less that poor single mothers are poor than that they are single.

Claiming that "immorality, promiscuity, and unwed motherhood seemed to be rewarded and encouraged by the easy allowance made upon a simple application of need,"[5] policymakers during the 1940s and '50s devised moral means tests as mechanisms for transferring mothers' dependency from government to men. By 1960, half the states limited assistance to "morally fit" mothers of children in "suitable homes." In some states, applicants were required to pledge "not to have any male callers coming into my home nor meeting me elsewhere under improper conditions . . . and to not knowingly contribute or be a contributing factor to [my children] being shamed for my conduct. I understand that should I violate this agreement, the children will be taken from me."[6] In Georgia beginning in the early 1950s, state policy directed welfare workers to scrutinize non-marital children's homes to assess their suitability. In Mississippi beginning in 1958, state policy denied welfare to all children whose parents were not ceremonially married.[7] In Louisiana and Mississippi, non-marital mothers were subject to criminal penalties (incarceration or a fine) for having borne children outside marriage. In most states, welfare agencies could end non-marital motherhood among recipients by sterilizing them.[8]

Alongside measures that punished poor mothers for their marital condition at childbirth, policymakers also developed rules requiring that biological fathers fulfill the traditional paternal provider role, whether or not they had ever been married to the mothers of their children. In 1950, Congress took a first stab at enforcing mothers' economic dependence on biological fathers by requiring welfare officials to notify law enforcement whenever a fatherless child enrolled in Aid to Families with Dependent Children (AFDC). In each of its welfare reform intiatives since 1967, Congress has insisted that recipient mothers must disclose the identity of their children's fathers; in 1974, it made maternal cooperation in the establishment of paternity a condition of receiving welfare. Since 1974, the paternity establishment provision has been accompanied by increasingly stringent measures to enforce child support, which codified the expectation that biological fathers, not government, ought to provide economically for poor single mothers and their children.

At the state level beginning in the 1940s and at the national level beginning in the 1960s, welfare reformers also were eager to require certain recipients either to replace or to combine welfare with wages. In part, policymakers promoted work requirements as a way to control welfare caseloads and welfare costs. But they also imposed work requirements as an instrument of moral apartheid, to punish poor mothers for the economic effects of their marital and reproductive choices.[9] While schools, the media, employers, and politicians all encouraged married mothers to remain in the home raising children during the 1950s and '60s, welfare administrators pushed unmarried, mostly Black mothers into the labor market. Marriage drew the line between moral worlds, and served as a proxy for racial distinctions as well. Those mothers who fell on the wrong side of the line were expected to atone in the fields, in factories, or in other women's homes. By the late 1960s, reformers pursued work requirements as a solution to a welfare crisis they defined as the chronic dependency of chronically unmarried Black mothers. Summoning images of lazy matriarchs on the dole, policymakers proposed outside work as the route to improved personal behavior—punishing "welfare chiselers," harnessing "brood mares," and giving "matriarchs" incentive to marry. Work provisions provided a way to avoid paying the wrong women to stay at home with children born under the wrong conditions; wage work became penance for illegitimacy.

Led by House Ways and Means Committee chair Wilbur Mills (D-Arkansas), national welfare reformers borrowed from the states the idea that welfare policy should encourage or require recipients to work outside the home. Local rules developed in the 1940s and '50s defined some welfare applicants, usually women of color, as "employable mothers" whose ability to work for wages disqualified them from welfare.[10] Mills's home state of Arkansas, for example, terminated grants to mothers it deemed employable at planting or harvest time.[11] Other rules made wage work a condition of welfare eligibility.[12] By 1962, thirty-one states had some form of work requirement on the books. But the decision to link work and welfare did not bespeak an unqualified consensus supporting wage-earning for all mothers, or even for all welfare mothers, especially when young children were involved.[13] For example, even as state-level work requirements proliferated during the 1950s, the national *Handbook of Public Assistance* maintained that welfare should "make it possible for a mother to choose between staying at home to care for her children and taking a job."[14]

From the 1960s to the present, work provisions in national welfare policy have equivocated about recipient mothers' work outside the home, mandating maternal employment in principle while exempting mothers of young children and emphasizing the wage work obligations of fathers. Moreover, federal work provisions usually have anticipated domesticity, not wage-earning, from mothers with husbands, either relaxing or relieving work requirements for mothers in two-parent families that were eligible for AFDC. Even under the Personal Responsibility Act of 1996, marriage constitutes an alternative to—or perhaps a form of—employment for mothers, immunizing them from the obligation to work outside the home.

The first federal work initiative, the Public Welfare Amendments of 1962, permitted states to condition welfare eligibility on participation in community work and training programs, but exempted mothers of children under age six. The policy also made benefits available to unemployed fathers in two-parent families, thus enabling their wives to sustain their caregiving work in the home.[15] By contrast, the Work Incentive Program (WIN) set up by the Social Security Act Amendments of 1967 permitted states to require all employable mothers to register for or participate in work training programs, regardless of the ages of their children. But the only persons whom the federal policy *required* states to refer to work programs were "appropriate" persons over age sixteen; implementing regulations required that unemployed fathers and children over age sixteen who were no longer in school be given priority for WIN training and jobs.[16] Despite the fact that women headed 90 percent of AFDC families, 38 percent of WIN participants in 1971 were men; the following year, women still made up only 53 percent of the program. This preference for masculine employment marked a victory for welfare recipients, many of whom fiercely resisted compulsory work outside the home. But it also reflected policymakers' support for marital families headed by breadwinning men. At the 1970 hearings on the Family Assistance Plan, a Nixon administration official explained why mothers in marital families need not work outside the home: "Where there are two [parents] present it is more like a normal family in the sense that the emphasis is on the father, the emphasis on upgrading and career development for him to get him into a better paying job, and to pull him out of the welfare program entirely so he becomes entirely self-supporting. The mother role becomes one of supporting the family, caring for the children while he is trying to improve his income."[17]

Congress revisited the WIN program in 1971 with the aim of strengthening its work requirements. Hearings revealed continued uncertainty about requiring wage work of all mothers. The 1971 Talmadge Amendments, though more severe in their treatment of recipients deemed eligible for employment, again excluded from the work requirement both single mothers of children under age six and married mothers with employable husbands in the home (regardless of the ages of their children). Further, the revised WIN program retained priority for program participation for unemployed fathers, followed by dependent children over age sixteen and then by mothers who volunteered to participate. These provisions reiterated the presumption that fathers, not mothers, should provide for their families.

The idea that fathers were the solution to maternal and child poverty reflected the masculine bias of Great Society employment programs such as the Job Corps, which typically excluded women from job training by assigning men higher priority for program slots. The idea also summarized the moral purpose of welfare reform: namely, to restore the patriarchal marital family. Republicans embraced this goal along with Democrats, only more so.

During the early 1970s, Republicans proposed reorienting welfare away from poor single mothers and toward poor but breadwinning husbands. Introduced by Richard Nixon in the summer of 1969, the Family Assistance Plan (FAP) offered a guaranteed annual income to all poor families with children; however, its income formula favored families with a wage-earning parent. Following Daniel Patrick Moynihan's warning that "a community that allows a large number of young men to grow up in broken families, dominated by women . . . asks for and gets chaos,"[18] FAP proponents pitched the policy to low-wage men. Promising men priority in job training and structuring benefits to reward wage work by fathers, FAP "assure[d] that the family of a working man will always be better off than a family of the same size headed by a man who is not working."[19] Providing benefits to each of two parents in a household while capping family earnings, FAP further subsidized the wives of low-wage men when they remained at home to care for their children. The FAP benefits formula tacitly directed poor single mothers to marriage; work requirements for heads of households, whether single or married, punished solo mothers for parenting alone.

The Family Assistance Plan died in the Senate in 1972, and with it any serious consideration of a guaranteed annual income. But FAP's interior principles—work, not welfare; marriage, not dependency—guided welfare reform into the 1990s.

The 1981 Omnibus Budget Reconciliation Act strengthened work provisions by requiring certain recipients to work off their benefits—workfare. By 1988, welfare policy expected poor single mothers to work outside the home; it did not expect outside work of married mothers, even if poor. Under the Family Support Act (FSA) of that year, the Job Opportunity and Basic Skills (JOBS) program specifically conditioned welfare eligibility on the single mother's participation in work, education, or employment-related training programs. While the FSA continued the practice of exempting mothers of infants and toddlers from work requirements, it also contained a child care entitlement for recipient mothers of pre-school-age children, which required states to provide child care if a mother could not participate in employment, education, or training activities without it. In addition, the FSA required states to extend one year of transitional child care benefits to care-givers who left welfare to seek wages. The FSA's various provisions— particularly the one guaranteeing surrogate care for welfare mothers' children—codified the assumption that poor single mothers *should* work outside the home.[20]

Obliging mothers without husbands to work outside the home, the FSA's child care, job training, and work requirement provisions broke new ground. Indeed, according to its author, Senator Daniel Patrick Moynihan, the FSA transformed welfare from an income maintenance program for poor families into a temporary substitute for wages: "Receiving income support is no longer to be a permanent or even extended condition, but rather, a transition to employment and an immediate gain of parental support for children."[21]

But although the FSA clearly defined welfare as a stepping-stone to self-sufficiency through wages, it left open the question of *whose* wages a care-giver and her children were to depend on. The FSA did not expect married mothers to earn their own wages, for example, as it exempted one parent in two-parent families from participation in the mandatory work program unless states opted to require it from the second parent. Moreover, the FSA did not address the labor market inequalities that left about half of single-mother families below the poverty line in 1994 and that continue to deprive poor women of wages high enough to support children on their own. Hence, even as the FSA told poor single mothers to get a job, it did not provide the means for them to achieve economic independence through a job. In addition, while the FSA did provide funds for training, education, and social supports that might have enhanced the wage prospects of recipients, states often did not fully spend the funds.[22] As a result, although many mothers exited welfare for stretches under the FSA, many returned when low wages, no benefits, and inadequate child care put the well-being of their children at risk.

Ultimately, the FSA anchored the self-sufficiency of families in a paternal income. Upon signing it into law, President Reagan declared that the FSA "responds to my call in my 1986 State of the Union Message for real welfare reform—reform that will lead to lasting emancipation from welfare dependency. . . . *First*, the legislation improves our system for securing support from an absent parent."[23] With its emphasis on fathers, the FSA invigorated rather than transformed twenty years of welfare policy. Reiterating the long-standing patriarchal moral goal of welfare reform, the FSA's extensive child support and paternity establishment provisions connected mothers' independence from welfare to their dependence on the biological fathers of their children. Extending and expanding the Child Support Enforcement Act, these provisions included automatic wage attachments in all new or modified child support orders; interstate enforcement of child support orders; mandatory notation of parental social security numbers on birth certificates; mandatory establishment of paternity; and projects to improve non-custodial parents' access to their children.[24] They expressed a strong bipartisan consensus that fathers should pay for their families regardless of whether mothers and children desired relationships with them.[25]

The decades-old welfare reform campaign culminated in 1996 with the repeal of AFDC. In its place, Congress enacted Block Grants for Temporary Assistance for Needy Families (TANF) as Title I of the Personal Responsibility and Work Opportunity Reconciliation Act. Though both touted and feared as a major upheaval in social policy, the PRA's welfare provision is in some respects no more than a very strident echo of previous reforms. With its combined emphasis on heterosexual two-parent families and on work outside the home, the PRA embodies the goals and assumptions that have controlled welfare reform since the 1960s. It does this with a familiar attack on the choices that poor single mothers make for their families and about their own lives.

As the welfare title of the PRA makes clear in its statement of purpose, its goal is to promote marriage, marital parenting, and paternal support.[26] Thus the PRA extends the inveterate moral prescriptivity of welfare policy, and to back up its prescriptions it provides the economic sanction of work outside the home. The PRA does not actually compel mothers to marry, but its work requirement gives them strong incentive to do so. Mothers who do not marry may receive cash assistance but in exchange must leave their homes either to perform community service or to work for wages. A mother who wants to meet her care-giving obligations in the home would thus be wise to trade her welfare check for a husband's income. The sixty-month lifetime limit on welfare eligibility reinforces this logic, as loss of benefits, like work requirements, forces single mothers to forswear care-giving for wage-earning.[27]

If the punitive moralism of the PRA's welfare provision has a familiar ring, many of its administrative and regulatory details are more distinctive. For example, in a throwback to the century before 1870, when each state set its own immigration policies and determined the political and legal status of its noncitizen residents, the PRA delegates to each state discretion (also known as a "state option") to decide whether noncitizen residents can ever be eligible for TANF.[28] In more widely heralded moves, the PRA withdraws the welfare entitlement for qualified care-givers and children, while shoring up states' rights over welfare policy through block grants and through stringent restrictions on the federal government's regulatory oversight of state welfare (TANF) programs.[29] But even as the PRA expands state discretion over welfare eligibility, spending, and administration, it conditions each state's entitlement to federal funds on its implementation of national moral standards.

## Welfare before Rights

Throughout this century, moralism has been the template for welfare policy and politics. Sometimes it has invoked strict canonical prescriptions for virtue and sanctions for sin. But more typically it has enforced the race, class, and gender order, conflating virtue with obedience to white, middle-class, patriarchal rules and with conformity to the dominant culture's ways of doing things.

Welfare was designed more than eighty years ago as an income alternative to a market wage for solo mothers, so that they could work in the home raising their own children. But not all needy mothers received benefits. Through eligibility rules and administrative stipulations, early twentieth-century welfare policy conditioned income support on the moral worthiness and cultural assimilation of poor single mothers. In many northern and eastern cities, European immigrant mothers without breadwinning husbands often surrendered cultural autonomy and family privacy in exchange for economic support. Across the country, but especially in the South and West, women of color were customarily regarded as inherently unfit and ineducable and hence were denied benefits.[30]

Known as mothers' pensions, early welfare was enacted by state governments and implemented by localities. Though states' policies varied, most shared common purposes and assumptions. In principle, mothers' pensions honored the care-giving work of mothers while discriminating among types of mothers in practice. Pensions provided economic support to "the best" mother-workers, while regulating the cultural conditions under which such mothers did their jobs. They defined mothers' care-giving work as socially productive, but only if care-givers met certain cultural and moral standards. Thus from its inception welfare policy foregrounded differences among mothers, equating cultural conformity with maternal worthiness, and so inscribed debates about women and welfare with the idiom of culture and character.

The most enduring legacy of early initiatives is that poor mothers earned their benefits by submitting to social controls. This legacy was carried over into the New Deal version of mothers' pensions—the Aid to Dependent Children program. Created by the Social Security Act of 1935, ADC (later renamed Aid to Families with Dependent Children, or AFDC) nationalized mothers' pension policies by providing for joint federal-state funding of welfare benefits and by requiring states to hew to certain administrative rules in exchange for federal dollars. Though the welfare measure—Title IV of the Social Security Act—abjured moral criteria, basing eligibility for benefits on need alone, it gave states the opportunity to impose moral criteria by delegating administration and management to them.[31] States took old rules from mothers' pension programs—rules against non-marital motherhood and heterosexual cohabitation, for example—and folded them into the new federal policy.

States claimed wide discretion to condition welfare benefits on moral worthiness as well as to decide whom they would make benefits available to and on what terms. Some states exercised this discretion more aggressively than others: southern states, for example, were notorious for imposing moral means tests on welfare participation by African American women. Unhampered by muscular federal instructions to treat all poor single mothers equally, many states continued the practice of distinguishing widows as presumptively worthy, giving them priority, if not exclusive eligibility, for benefits.

At least initially, welfare did not disturb the racial status quo while it invigorated local governments' patriarchal moral leverage over poor women. States continued to control access to welfare, as well as the power to police recipients. Not surprisingly, welfare recipients in 1939 were overwhelmingly (89 percent) white, notwithstanding the racially disparate distribution of poverty.[32]

A 1939 amendment to the Social Security Act, however, exploded the established order. The amendment created the survivors' insurance system, providing income support to the widows and children of male workers whose wages and occupations qualified them to participate in the system. Unlike welfare, survivors' benefits were nationally standardized and automatically disbursed. So long as a husband paid into the system, and so long as a widow cared for minor children and did not remarry, the national government would send her a monthly stipend so that she could attend to the work of care-giving.[33]

With this policy change, welfare, once the income policy for worthy widows and their children, lost its only venerated constituency. Worthy widows, who were 61 percent of ADC mothers in 1939, were mostly white; always mothers of marital children; and blameless survivors of stable marriages to regularly employed, socially insured men. The departure of widows from welfare—only 7.7 percent of welfare mothers were widows by 1961—transformed welfare into a safety net for morally disdained, racially despised women. Divorced, deserted, or never married, "welfare mothers" could now be blamed for their single motherhood: perhaps they drove their husbands away; obviously they had weak family values; undoubtedly they were oversexed and promiscuous; by definition they were matriarchs. With the application of such stigma, even the few widows who remained in ADC lost their legitimacy: they had been married to the wrong men, usually men of color, who, because of income or occupation (often both) were excluded from the social insurance system and so could not provide survivors' benefits for their familes.

Some states responded to the evacuation of widows from welfare by raising the moral hurdles to welfare participation. Many states developed or strengthened such moral conditions as "substitute father," "man-in-the-house," and "suitable home" rules. Many states also introduced work requirements, contravening welfare's stated goal of making it economically feasible for poor single mothers to work inside the home caring for their children. First promulgated in Louisiana in 1943, work requirements ("employable mother" rules) declared some women more suitable as workers than as mothers. An inverted means test of sorts, the Louisiana measure allowed welfare agencies to deny assistance to poor mothers if they could earn wages by working in the fields. Racially targeted in application against African American women and Latinas, early work requirements underscored the social disapprobation of poor women of color who parented alone.[34]

Eligibility rules had always sifted "deserving" from "undeserving" single mothers. The departure of socially approved single mothers to the survivors' insurance system shifted the emphasis of eligibility rules, for now most welfare mothers were morally suspect. Where the rules had once worked to identify the worthy and uplift them to "American" habits and values, now they were focused against despised women either to punish them or to deprive them of benefits. Nonetheless, women of color entered the welfare system in disproportionate numbers, a reflection of their disproportionate poverty. By 1961, African American families accounted for 44 percent of the welfare caseload.[35] This shift called into question the premise of welfare, as women of color, long held in opposition to Anglo American feminine and maternal ideals, were now major beneficiaries of a program originally designed to reward Anglo American maternal domesticity.

Through the 1940s and '50s, states had substantial discretion over welfare programs. Beginning in 1960, however, the federal government began to set firmer standards for the conduct of state programs. In that year, the Social Security Administration argued that as a constitutional matter, states could not exclude non-marital mothers and children from welfare participation.[36] Further, in 1961 the federal government invalidated Louisiana's "suitable home" regulation, which defined as unsuitable any home in which a non-marital child was born to a mother receiving welfare. Enforcing this regulation, Louisiana had expunged 23,000 children from AFDC during the summer of 1960, 95 percent of whom were Black.[37] In a crucial decision, Arthur Flemming, secretary of Health, Education, and Welfare, ruled that states could "not impose an eligibility condition that would deny assistance with respect to a needy child on the basis that the home conditions in which the child lives are unsuitable" unless efforts were made to improve home conditions or to remove the child to alternative care.[38] This ruling barred states from making marital motherhood a condition of AFDC eligibility. Congress gave statutory approval to the Flemming ruling in its 1961 and 1962 welfare amendments. Though the ruling invited states to police welfare families' home conditions to monitor their suitability, it also stalled state use of "suitable home" requirements to block welfare participation altogether.

Federal welfare administrators of the early 1960s did not definitively prohibit states from imposing moral restrictions on welfare eligibility, but their rulings began a process of expanding welfare and of regulating state programs. Social, political, and legal challenges to the many ways in which state welfare programs assaulted the rights and dignity of recipients created enormous pressures to democratize, regularize, and nationalize access to welfare benefits. The welfare rights movement, which began at the local level in 1963 and had ignited nationally by 1966, staked its claims before local welfare agencies and before the Supreme Court. By the late 1960s, recipients had won judicial recognition of the basic statutory and constitutional rights of welfare participants. The Court's affirmation of recipients' due process and entitlement protections constrained the states' discretionary moral control over welfare. By 1970, where welfare benefits had once been doled out to poor single mothers at the pleasure of local governments, they were now *owed* to all mothers who met either the specifications or intent of federal law. Where federal welfare policy's silence on moral issues had once given states a moral carte blanche, that silence now set limits on the power of state governments.

## States' Rights and Welfare Rights

Commentators repeatedly but erroneously have observed that the new welfare law ends a sixty-year federal guarantee of economic assistance for poor mothers and children. While the Personal Responsibility Act of 1996 does terminate a sixty-year-old *program*, the *guarantee* it rescinds has been available to poor mothers and children for only thirty years. This guarantee began to emerge in 1968, when, in *King v. Smith*, a unanimous Supreme Court struck down Alabama's substitute father rule.[39] An extrastatutory eligibility condition, the rule had disqualified some 16,000 children from AFDC when it was first promulgated—90 percent of whom were African Americans. Like man-in-the-house rules, the substitute father provision defined any able-bodied man with whom a needy mother was intimately associated as the de facto father of and presumptive provider for her children.[40] Finding the Alabama regulation in conflict with the federal statute, the Court prohibited states from denying "AFDC assistance to dependent children on the basis of their mothers' alleged immorality or to discourage illegitimate births."[41]

In *King*, the Court reasoned that the "paramount goal" of AFDC was the economic protection of children. Applying this logic to all state eligibility criteria, the Court suggested that state AFDC programs could not deny aid to *any* mothers and children eligible by need unless the federal law specifically authorized them to do so. Another unaminous decision elaborated this position in 1971, holding that "a state eligibility standard that excludes persons eligible for assistance under the federal AFDC standard violates the Social Security Act and is therefore invalid under the Supremacy Clause."[42]

A series of Supreme Court decisions established the welfare entitlement, but the entitlement did not establish a general right to receive welfare; for the Social Security Act did not require states to participate in the AFDC program. Nor did the Social Security Act require participating states to provide cash assistance or social services beyond what was "practicable under the conditions in [each] State."[43] Hence, even if a family had a claim to cash assistance because its state ran an AFDC program, the family did not have a claim to a specific level of assistance. What the federal welfare entitlement *did* provide, however, was a restraint on state eligibility standards, including standards that effectively taxed mothers' moral decisions by reducing, withholding, or terminating benefits. From *King* forward, states could deploy only such rules as were authorized by the federal statute.

The withdrawal of the states' discretionary control of welfare eligibility coincided with rapid and extensive growth of the AFDC caseload and with the mobilization by recipients of an unprecedented and determined welfare rights movement. In 1966, welfare rights groups from various states came together in the National Welfare Rights Organization. Through a combination of direct action and litigation, the movement elaborated a concept of welfare rights to fight the odious rules that impaired poor mothers' access to benefits and to ground political claims to economic assistance. Welfare rights litigation produced more liberal rules, and demonstrations at thousands of local welfare offices liberalized practices. Both developments increased participation in welfare.

From 1961 to 1971, enrolled individuals increased from 3.5 million to 11 million, with the number of recipients growing at an annual rate of almost 20 percent between 1967 and 1971. As the number of recipients grew, so did the number of people of color receiving benefits (although the proportion did not shift dramatically after 1958, hovering between 46 and 50 percent). With states like Louisiana and Alabama evicting Blacks from welfare in disproportionate numbers through moral fitness tests of one sort or another, with politicians denouncing never-married mothers as welfare chiselers, and with social scientists lamenting the structure of Black families needing welfare, the racial politics of welfare was clear.[44] As Elliot Richardson observed for the Nixon administration in 1970: "ominous racial overtones have developed, since current AFDC recipients—those who are helped—are about 50 percent nonwhite, while the working poor—those who are excluded—are about 70 percent white. This country can no longer afford to have one of its most important and needed antipoverty efforts viewed, by many of its citizens, as a divisive, unfair, and arbitrary failure."[45] Thus defined as a "Black" program and a "failure," welfare was poised for repeal.

Soaring costs sealed welfare's fate. AFDC expenditures rose with the increase in participation. Since national and state governments jointly financed AFDC, states acutely felt the fiscal effects of their increasing caseloads. But where states had once been able to invent their own eligibility criteria to control enrollments, by the late 1960s they were restrained from doing so. The combination of race, states' rights, and cost stoked the politics of welfare reform, rallying whites against Blacks, Congress against the Court, and taxpayers against recipients.

Between 1968 and 1975, the Supreme Court nationalized the political status of poor single mothers by extending rights to them. A few of these rights were rooted in the Constitution— the right to travel, for example, and the procedural guarantee of a fair hearing.[46] Most were construed from the Social Security Act. The Court determined, for instance, that the Act's AFDC provision established categorical welfare eligibility for poor care-givers and their children. This redefined welfare from discretionary relief to statutory entitlement. Constitutional rights are stronger and more durable than statutory rights, but this was a distinction without a difference for states eager to manage eligibility for welfare. The Court was careful to point out, however, even in *King v. Smith*, that AFDC was "a scheme of cooperative federalism."[47] On this basis it sustained some state and local welfare policies, such as New York's policy of sending welfare workers to recipients' homes[48] and Maryland's policy capping family benefits regardless of variations in family size.[49] In the main, though, the thrust of *King* and related decisions was to assert federal authority over state AFDC programs, especially over program rules that impaired participation by categorically eligible mothers and children. Following *King*, the Court struck down Connecticut's residency requirement;[50] California's man-in-the-house regulation;[51] New Jersey's rule limiting AFDC benefits to families where parents were legally married;[52] and New York's requirement that lodgers help with AFDC family rents, which reduced family benefits.[53]

As AFDC participants won protection through national rights, states' rights were compromised. Before the late 1960s, states had coupled to welfare administration a fairly expansive police power. They had been able to do this because of the decentralized structure of AFDC, which, unlike old-age and survivors' insurance, for example, explicitly required states to share funding burdens and to bear administrative responsibility. Until welfare administration was reined in by rights, states enjoyed considerable flexibility to condition welfare benefits on moral fitness and moral supervision.

States accumulated this flexibility not from AFDC policy

alone, but more importantly from the Tenth Amendment's delegation of power to the states. The "reserve clause" of the Constitution gave plenary regulatory authority to states over matters not specifically assigned to the federal government. Called the "police power," this legislative discretion entitles states to protect and promote health, safety, morals, and the general welfare. It is from the police power that the claim of states' rights flows; and it is through the police power that states historically have organized and maintained race and gender hierarchies. Indeed, through U. S. history state law has provided most of the weapons of racism and patriarchy: property law, electoral law, criminal law, and family law are all primarily determined by the states. Property law in southern states protected slavery until the Civil War. Electoral law disfranchised white women in most states until 1920 and African American women and men in southern states until the mid-1960s. Criminal law accepted the lynching of Black men by white and today still delivers racially disparate prosecutions and punishment. Meanwhile, family law in all states subordinated the decisional, sexual, and property rights of wives to the absolute prerogatives of husbands until the 1970s. Even though the prerogative of husbands has diminished in recent decades, state governments retain control over women's most intimate experiences—sex, marriage, divorce, custody, and family violence.[54]

Beginning with the New Deal, but especially since the 1960s, exclusive state authority in these areas bowed to constitutional interests. From the mid-1950s into the early 1970s, judicial decisions and congressional actions held the police power delegated to states under the Tenth Amendment accountable to the constitutional protections guaranteed to individuals under the Bill of Rights and Fourteenth Amendment. As a result, the states' right to segregate African Americans in separate schools, for example, or routinely exclude women from jury duty, fell before the individual's right to equal protection under the law. This process both universalized and nationalized citizenship, even where the Constitution or Congress had awarded some discretion to the states.

Judicial reasoning about welfare followed this new framework for national citizenship, scrutinizing the actions of state governments in terms of their consequences for the national rights of individuals. In two seminal welfare decisions, the Court subordinated state rules to constitutional rights: residency requirements fell before the fundamental right to travel (*Shapiro v. Thompson*), and summary termination of benefits fell before Fourteenth Amendment due process guarantees (*Goldberg v. Kelly*). In most other welfare cases, however, the Supreme Court measured state policies and practices against its understanding of the words and intent of the federal welfare statute. Repeatedly finding that the Social Security Act imposed only two requirements for AFDC eligibility—need and dependency—the Court withdrew the states' prerogative to augment federal requirements with moral conditions and thereby restrict access to welfare.

The Court's limitations on states' discretionary rights over welfare focused the attention of welfare foes on changing the federal welfare statute. Blaming the Supreme Court for "this great big welfare mess" and for "the phenomenal growth of the welfare rolls in the last three years," Senate Finance Committee chair Russell Long (D-Louisiana) complained: "Common to many of these cases seems to be an assumption that welfare is a 'property right' rather than a 'gratuity' granted as a privilege by the Congress and subject to such eligibility conditions as the Congress, through the legislative process, decides to impose." Long was reacting to judicial reasoning that culminated in the Supreme Court's *Goldberg* ruling in March 1970. Writing for the

*Goldberg* majority, Justice Brennan found that "public assistance, then, is not mere charity, but a means to 'promote the
general Welfare, and secure the Blessings of Liberty to ourselves and our Posterity.' The same governmental interests that
counsel the provision of welfare, counsel as well its uninter-
rupted provision to those eligible to receive it."[55] Moreover,
embracing legal scholars' theories of "the new property," Brennan noted that "it may be realistic today to regard welfare
entitlements as more like 'property' than a 'gratuity.' Much of
the existing wealth in this country takes the form of rights that
do not fall within traditional common-law concepts of property."[56] Quoting Charles Reich, the leading theorist of the new
property, Brennan continued: "Society today is built around
entitlement. . . . Many of the most important of these entitlements now flow from government: subsidies to farmers and
businessmen; routes for airlines and channels for television
stations; long term contracts for defense, space, and education;
social security pensions for individuals. Such sources of security, whether private or public, are no longer regarded as
luxuries or gratuities; to the recipients they are essentials, fully
deserved, and in no sense a form of charity."[57]

Long used his power over legislation to fight the Court's
liberalization of welfare. In 1970, he proposed amendments to
welfare policy to make clear that "the 'right to welfare' is a
statutory right, dependent on legislation enacted by the Congress and . . . can be extended, restricted, altered, amended, or
even repealed by the Congress." Accordingly, the welfare
amendments of 1970 aimed to circumvent judicial decisions by
adding to the federal welfare law eligibility criteria previously
determined by states: residency requirements, man-in-the-
house rules, mandatory establishment of paternity, and home
visits.[58] Had they survived a Senate filibuster, many of these

provisions effectively would have federalized the police power by nationalizing the moral contingency of welfare.

Long's efforts in 1970 were part of a series of congressional initiatives that had begun in 1967 to add moralistic provisions to the federal welfare statute. In what Daniel Patrick Moynihan at the time called "the first purposively punitive welfare legislation in the history of American national government,"[59] the 1967 welfare amendments sought to accomplish what suitable home and illegitimacy sanctions had achieved until the 1961 Flemming ruling stemmed their effects: the expulsion from the welfare rolls of despised women and their children. In addition to creating the WIN program, the amendments took aim against never-married mothers and their children by requiring the establishment of paternity for all enrolled children. The amendments also penalized mother-only families by freezing appropriations for them—a precocious version of the 1996 block grants to states. Congress repealed the freeze before it could go into effect, however.

The welfare rights movement deserves much credit for the repeal, in part because of the rights it won for recipients in 1968 and 1969. The Court's decision in *Shapiro v. Thompson*, drew particular congressional attention. *Shapiro* linked the constitutional right to travel to welfare participation, finding the states' residency requirement for welfare to be an invidious classification that "chill[s] the assertion of constitutional rights by penalizing those who choose to exercise them."[60] The Court's strong protection of the "basic right" to travel against the states' interest in deterring the in-migration of poor people foiled Congress's attempt to reform welfare and control program growth among unmarried mothers by capping federal expenditures. The Senate Finance Committee balked; removal of residency controls on welfare participation, it concluded, would swell welfare caseloads in many states. But short of amending the Constitution to reverse the Court's ruling in *Shapiro*, Congress's hands were tied. If it had not repealed the freeze on federal appropriations, states would have been stuck with the full costs of hundreds of thousands of new AFDC enrollments. This was too big a price to ask the states to pay for engineering marital parenthood in welfare families.

Ways and Means Committee chair Wilbur Mills had hoped that the 1967 amendments would end "welfare as a way of life." From his point of view and that of Russell Long and other conservatives, this goal was sabotaged by the Court. The Court respected the statutory language and legislative history of AFDC policy, even as the statute changed: it affirmed the federal work requirement enacted in 1967, for example, while treating it as a floor, rather than a ceiling, for state work programs.[61] But the Court's literal reading of the federal statute stymied new reform initiatives. Chief among these were mandatory paternity establishment and child support enforcement provisions. These initiatives arose in response to popular complaints that welfare encouraged illegitimacy by rewarding mothers who bore children outside of marriage and permitting fathers to abandon their children. Both initiatives responded also to the main effect of *King v. Smith*, which was to bar states from arbitrarily assigning financial responsibility for children to the male lover or friend of a poor single mother; *King* left the door open, however, to state assertion of biological fathers' legal duty to support their children. Paternity establishment would determine who the fathers of AFDC children were; child support enforcement would turn such fathers into breadwinners for AFDC children and mothers.

Still, so long as the federal welfare law tied AFDC eligibility to economic rather than moral criteria, the Court would look askance at state efforts to use the new paternity establishment provision to screen welfare participation. Accordingly, the Court affirmed, between 1969 and 1973, fifteen lower court decisions striking down state regulations that made paternity establishment a condition of welfare eligibility.[62]

Even though the 1967 welfare amendments mandated paternity establishment, they did not specifically tie it to a mother's receipt of cash assistance. In fact, though the 1967 measure required states to improve paternity establishment programs, it did not compel mothers to cooperate. Nor did the law mention any consequences for the children of mothers who did not comply. As in *Doe v. Shapiro*, courts accordingly argued that "although the state argues with considerable force that the Social Security Act requires it to take affirmative steps to ascertain paternity in the case of illegitimate children receiving AFDC assistance, we do not think that [the 1967 provision] was ever intended to allow a state to disqualify an otherwise eligible child."[63] Under these circumstances, to reestablish moral leverage in welfare policy would require redefining welfare's purpose as well as the conditions of eligibility.

In its report accompanying the unsuccessful 1970 welfare amendments, the Senate Finance Committee responded to *Doe v. Shapiro*: "A recent court decision held that a mother's refusal to name the father of her illegitimate child could not result in denial of aid to families with dependent children. . . . The committee's bill would clarify congressional intent by specifying that the requirement that welfare be furnished 'promptly' may not preclude a state from seeking the aid of a mother in identifying the father of a child born out of wedlock."[64] At Senate welfare hearings in 1971, conservatives voiced their resolve to reestablish the pre-*King* moral regime even more strongly. In the context of *King* and its progeny, however, that regime would be restored at the expense of states' rights—through the clear specification of federal standards.

During the 1971 hearings, Senator Long repeatedly flogged the Court for acting "contrary to the will of Congress" and for "very erroneously and incorrectly" refusing to derive financial responsibility from a relationship between a man and an AFDC mother.[65] Doubting that Congress could fix the "welfare mess" by reversing the Supreme Court's interpretation of the AFDC statute, Long called for changing the law to direct the Court's future interpretation. At the top of his list of changes was the conscription of biological fathers into poor mother-headed families. Seeing paternity establishment and child support as the way to accomplish what substitute father and man-in-the-house rules once did, Long urged "making papa admit to the paternity of his own child and do something about it."[66] This would restore the marital family economy, if not marital family life, and shift the burden of family support from government to fathers.

Responding to judicial skepticism about existing paternity establishment provisions, Congress fundamentally altered welfare in 1974 by making a mother's cooperation in the establishment of paternity a condition of welfare participation. In 1984, 1988, and again in 1996, Congress toughened paternity and child support conditions, firmly claiming for the federal government the moral gatekeeping once performed by states.

During the 1970s and '80s, national welfare reforms added other eligibility conditions. By the early 1990s, a single mother not only had to be needy but also had to cooperate in establishing the paternity of her child and in obtaining child support payments; had to assign child and spousal support rights to the state; had to identify third parties, including fathers, who might bear responsibility for her child's health care expenses; had to participate in the JOBS program; and could not be on strike.[67]

These developments did not affect the statutory purpose of welfare, however, which was to provide economic support for poor children and their care-givers. Even the work-oriented Family Support Act retained the core goal of AFDC: "encouraging the care of dependent children in their own homes . . . by enabling each State to furnish financial assistance and rehabilitation and other services . . . to needy dependent children and the parents or relatives with whom they are living to maintain and strengthen family life and to help such parents or relatives to attain or retain capability of the maximum self-support and personal independence *consistent with the maintenance of continuing parental care and protection.*"[68] So long as welfare law pledged support for care-giving to children, even while constraining it, welfare would not be fully reformed. Welfare "reform" in fact ultimately required its *repeal*, for the goal of reform since the 1960s had not been to improve economic assistance measures but to end poor mothers' need for them. The strategy for reform had been to end single motherhood itself or, failing that, to deny incorrigibly single mothers the right to work as care-givers for their own children.

## The End of Welfare

The Personal Responsibility Act ended welfare by withdrawing the Social Security Act's promise of economic assistance to poor care-givers and their children. During its first thirty years, various state restrictions on eligibility circumscribed AFDC's promise. During its second thirty years, a judicially defended national entitlement checked state restrictions. In response, Congress generated new national restrictions to either accomplish or authorize what states had once done on their own. But although new national eligibility conditions synchronized national and local moralistic interests, the new conditions also imposed additional procedural, administrative, and financial burdens on states. The new national eligibility conditions for individuals also became eligibility conditions for states participating in the AFDC program: states had to meet expensive federal requirements for child support enforcement and paternity establishment, for example, and had to mount work programs and provide child care. In addition, tethered to statutory interpretation from *King* forward, states could not be more morally restrictive than the welfare statute authorized—at least not without explicit permission in the form of waivers from the federal government.[69]

So even as national welfare policy grew more punitive toward recipients, cries for greater flexibility for the states intensified. The Personal Responsibility Act responded to some degree by authorizing states henceforth to be more restrictive than the law requires. Various "state options" restore state discretion: to compel mothers to work outside the home sooner than the federal law requires; to establish stricter time limits than the federal law requires; to strip families of cash benefits where mothers do not identify biological fathers; to withhold benefits to children born to mothers while enrolled on welfare; to sanction recipient families that include adults under age fifty-one who do not have and are not seeking a high school diploma; to declare all noncitizens ineligible for assistance; to require drug tests of recipients; to cut benefits to mothers whose children are truant; to treat new state residents under the welfare rules of their former state; and to provide no cash benefits at all.

At this writing, state welfare plans are far from set in stone. But so far New York City, Massachusetts, California, Florida, Tennessee, Texas, and Wisconsin compel mothers to work outside the home immediately upon receiving benefits; Wisconsin requires recipients to work longer hours than required by the federal law. Michigan reduces benefits by 25 percent if people do not meet work requirements within two months. Alabama, South Carolina, and Wyoming will not provide benefits to non-citizen immigrants. Nineteen of the forty states that had filed welfare plans with the Department of Health and Human Services by June, 1997 said they would impose the family cap. Meanwhile, twenty states have set shorter time limits than the federal law requires for all or part of their caseloads. For example, Utah has decided to limit lifetime welfare eligibility to three years even though the federal limit is five years; Indiana imposes a two-year lifetime limit; Florida restricts eligibility to no more than two years during any five-year period, with a lifetime limit of four years; Montana has a two-year limit, but only for single parents; Texas limits benefits to twelve months for recipients who have completed high school or who have worked outside the home at least eighteen months in the past; and California limits new recipients to eighteen months of consecutive benefits, with a lifetime limit of five years.[70]

Block grants and the recision of the entitlement strengthen the discretion of states. States are no longer obliged to provide assistance to *all* needy families, even if all of them meet state eligibility criteria. If funds run out, some needy families will have to go without. Nor must states provide assistance to equally needy families: they may declare noncitizens ineligible for benefits and may condition benefits or benefit levels on, say, the marital status of the mother. Further, each state need not administer its TANF program uniformly across its own political subdivisions,[71] so the income protection and social supports available to poor women and their children will vary according to where they live, even within one state.[72] In combination with block grants, which provide fixed, exhaustible sums to states, the end of the entitlement makes economic assistance both conditional (requiring conformity to rules set by each state) and unreliable (subject to the availability of funds).

The PRA's delegation of administrative and spending discretion over work programs and child care services further enhances state flexibility. So does its prohibition of federal regulation of state programs beyond the oversight expressly stipulated in the law. Still, the PRA promotes state flexibility within limits: each state must comply with a score of conditions in exchange for a block grant,[73] and no state may be less moralistic than the federal policy.

What's most distinctive about the PRA is the national government's unapologetic imposition of moral stipulations, its bold appropriation of the police power. Through a combination of incentives, requirements, and prohibitions, the PRA obligates states to enforce national moral standards governing intimate associations and decisions. At the top of the federal list of priorities is to discourage non-marital childbearing. Hence, to receive its TANF block grant, a state must document, in writing, its goals and strategies for reducing non-marital pregnancies and births and its plans to improve statutory rape enforcement.[74] As an incentive to fight illegitimacy, the PRA offers an annual federal bonus to the five states that rank highest in reducing non-marital births while also decreasing abortions.[75] An incentive is not a requirement, of course. But since the only way states can increase their inelastic block grants is through federal bonuses, they would be wise to comply. Hence, the PRA may induce states to make abortion even less accessible (longer waiting periods and more expensive medical requirements); to make contraception more compulsory (use of Norplant as a condition of cash assistance); and to impose legal sanctions on pre-marital sex and non-marital childbearing (fornication prosecutions and the family cap). Already, the PRA has inspired Utah to consider paying unmarried women $3000 bonuses if they complete their pregnancies and surrender their babies to adoption.[76]

Less widely discussed have been the requirements the law imposes on states in exchange for TANF funds. To participate in the new program, states must enforce federal mandatory establishment of paternity and child support enforcement rules, including the PRA's provision reducing or terminating benefits for families where the mother is deemed noncooperative.[77] This is not a toothless provision, as a state's failure to apply the PRA's penalty triggers a reduction in its TANF grant. Similarly, states are prohibited from providing assistance to unmarried mothers under age eighteen who have not completed high school and who are not engaged in an educational activity, as well as to unmarried mothers under age eighteen who do not live with a parent or guardian.[78] Meanwhile, states must enforce work requirements, must meet federal work participation rates, must adhere to federal definitions of work, and may not use federal funds to provide cash assistance to families for longer than sixty months.[79]

Though the PRA offers many options to states—thereby creating many dangers for individuals—it is far from a restoration of states' rights. A state *must* do certain things in exchange for its block grant. It also must *not* do certain things even if local majorities want to. A state cannot offer assistance on more generous or more equitable terms than are stipulated in the PRA. So, for example, if a state wants to treat teenage mothers uniformly, whether or not they are married, they can do so only by restricting the welfare eligibility of married teenage mothers, not by activating the eligibility of unmarried teenage mothers who are living on their own. If a state wants to use its block grant to provide cash assistance to families as long as they need it, it may not do so, even if its TANF funds exceed demand. If a state wants to suspend the work requirement, whether because remunerative employment is unavailable or because single mothers already have one job in the home, it would have to support recipients wholly on its own. By so restricting the use of federal funds, the PRA impedes some states' provision of the economic assistance required by their own constitutions: New York's, for example, promises that "aid, care and support of the needy are public concerns and shall be provided by the state."[80]

The PRA is, then, a moral straightjacket, conceived and enacted to disjoin rights from welfare and thus to intensify the disciplinary function of social policies affecting poor women. To accomplish both the economic disfranchisement and moral disciplining of poor single mothers, the PRA makes national government the source of rules governing intimate matters. Notwithstanding the Supreme Court's recent decision in *United States v. Lopez*, where both majority and dissent noted that family law is beyond the constitutional scope of the national government, Congress and the president have arrogated key elements of family law to regulate the marital, maternal, reproductive, and vocational choices of mothers who are single and poor.[81] That this was the purpose of welfare reform is nowhere better stated than in the PRA's preamble. The first paragraph of the Act begins: "Marriage is the foundation of a successful society." After enumerating a score of "negative consequences" for mothers, children, and society that flow from a mother's unmarried status, the Act redefines the purpose of welfare: "1) to provide assistance to needy families so that children may be cared for in their own homes or in the homes of relatives; 2) to end the dependence of needy parents on government benefits by promoting job preparation, work, and marriage; 3) to prevent and reduce the incidence of out-of-wedlock pregnancies and establish annual numerical goals for preventing and reducing the incidence of these pregnancies; and 4) to encourage the formation and maintenance of two-parent families."[82]

Three of the four statutory purposes of welfare policy henceforth involve promoting marriage rather than mitigating need. Three of the four statutory purposes of welfare now tie a single mother's economic security to her relationship with her child's father. Three of the four statutory purposes of welfare call upon states to infringe or withhold such rights as marital privacy, associational liberty, reproductive choice, and vocational freedom from poor women who are parenting alone.

In the remainder of this essay, I will examine the implications of the Personal Responsibility Act for the autonomy and equality rights of poor single mothers. My purpose is to highlight rights that the PRA invades and rights that might hold the PRA at bay. AFDC policy after *King* relied on "a scheme of cooperative federalism," wherein the Court invoked the national rights of individuals as a check against state governments' regulatory intrusions into recipients' lives. In a seismic paradigm shift, if one thirty years in the making, the PRA announces a new federal partnership joining national and state powers in regulating the lives of poor women. If unchallenged, this political consolidation of moralistic authority will disable poor single mothers' citizenship, deepen inequalities among women, and derail progress toward gender justice.

# 3

## Disdained Mothers, Unequal Citizens

### Paternity Establishment, Child Support,

### and the Stratification of Rights

onverging at the moral flash point of "illegitimacy," policymakers of the 1990s in both political parties made the
marital family economy a cornerstone of welfare reform.
Republicans emphasized the moral necessity of marriage and
sought sanctions against out-of-wedlock childbirth. Democrats
stressed the economic role of fathers and worked to strengthen
enforcement of their financial responsibility for families. Both
parties insisted that although mothers cannot be forced into
formal marriages, men can be forced to act like husbands and
fathers by providing for their children. Accordingly, aggressive
paternity establishment and tough pursuit of child support
were key provisions of the welfare bill proposed by President
Clinton in 1994, as well as of the Personal Responsibility Act
passed by the Republican Congress in 1996. These provisions
compel mothers who need welfare to cooperate in identifying,
tracking down, and collecting money from their children's fathers. They compel poor single mothers to surrender basic constitutional rights of associational freedom and reproductive
privacy as a condition of receiving economic assistance for their
families.

Paternity establishment and child support provisions received little critical attention during the debate over the PRA, in part because the idea of "making fathers pay" is broadly popular, even among groups that voiced opposition to the Republican bill on other grounds. These provisions were also overshadowed by the Republicans' zeal for punishing non-marital childbearing by making children born to mothers on welfare ineligible for benefits and making unmarried teenage mothers and their children ineligible, as well. The Republicans' most ruthless penalties for non-marital childbearing did not become law, however. The PRA permits states to impose a family cap but does not require them to do so, and it allows unmarried teenage mothers to receive welfare payments if they live under adult supervision.[1]

Ironically, the politics of reproductive choice helps explain this lapse in the conservative welfare agenda: many antichoice Republicans feared that stringent rules against non-marital childbearing would lead unmarried pregnant girls and women to seek abortions.[2] They also worried that the Act's provision for bonus payments to states whose non-marital birth rates decline most sharply might benefit states with permissive abortion policies. Hence, the Act stipulates that only states that reduce their abortion rates will be eligible to be rewarded for improved "illegitimacy ratios."[3] Unable to prevent non-marital childbearing outright, Republicans joined Democrats to simulate father-mother family structures through paternity establishment and child support for non-marital children.

Undoubtedly some Republicans would have liked to coerce mothers into marriage, either by denying welfare benefits to non-marital children or by requiring marriage as an ongoing condition of receiving benefits. However, constitutional doctrine protects the reproductive decisions of individuals whether or not they are married,[4] and it defends children against invidious distinctions based on their mothers' marital status at the time of their birth. For thirty years, the Supreme Court has overturned laws that treat children born into or raised in mother-only families differently from marital children.[5] According to the Court, laws that distinguish between marital and non-marital children are offensive not only because they discriminate against non-marital children on the basis of circumstances beyond their control, but also because they use those children to regulate the choices of their parents: "penalizing the illegitimate child is an ineffectual—as well as unjust—way of deterring the parent."[6] The Court's jurisprudence on illegitimacy has guarded certain child support and inheritance rights of non-marital children whose fathers have acknowledged them.[7] It has ensured the rights of non-marital families to welfare as well: in 1973, the Court definitively announced that states may not limit welfare only to families in which parents are "ceremonially married."[8] Given these constitutional constraints, conservatives had to settle for welfare stipulations that encourage marriage rather than require it—that foster marriage-like heterosexual family relationships rather than mandate formal unions.

The Personal Responsibility Act thus does not impose firm and direct national restrictions on non-marital child*bearing*. But it does attach stringent national conditions to non-marital child-*rearing* by poor mothers who need welfare. Under the provision for mandatory establishment of paternity, welfare eligibility depends upon a mother's willingness to reveal the identity of her child's father.[9] Since the purpose of paternity establishment is to assign child support obligations to biological fathers, the provision also requires a mother to cooperate in establishing, modifying, and enforcing the support order for her child. The law gives a state the option to exempt a mother from the cooperation requirements when it determines such an exemption is in the best interest of the child. This could relieve some families of the provisions' worst burden, namely exposure to abusive biological fathers. If experience is any guide, however, the degree of relief may not be great: less than one percent of welfare applicants claimed the "good cause" exemption under the old welfare law, often because of concerns about privacy and confidentiality. Fewer women may claim or receive "good cause" exemptions under the PRA, for unlike AFDC, which established national definitions for "good cause," TANF (the new welfare system) leaves it to states to define the scope and standards of the exemption.[10]

The 1996 welfare law completes a trend, rather than breaking new ground, for to some degree, mandatory maternal cooperation in paternity establishment and child support has been a feature of welfare policy since 1968. Increment by increment over the past thirty years, policymakers have stiffened requirements for maternal cooperation. Once the Supreme Court forbade states to impose or expect child support from a welfare mother's male lover if he was not her child's father, Congress moved swiftly to identify fathers upon whom it could impose a legal duty of support.[11]

Where mothers were not married, Congress derived paternal obligations from men's biological connection to children. This could not be determined, however, without information from mothers, nor could fathers be forced to pay for children without information from mothers about how to track them down. Hence, the welfare policy changes that took effect in 1968 required states to initiate paternity proceedings and expected maternal compliance. The 1974 Child Support Act made maternal cooperation a condition of receiving welfare payments, and the 1984 Child Support Amendments federalized the statute of limitations for paternity establishment so that non-marital mothers would be mandated to cooperate regardless of the ages of their minor children. To encourage mothers to cooperate, the 1984 measure permitted them to keep $50 of the monthly child support payments states collected from fathers. Then in 1988, the Family Support Act strengthened the maternal cooperation provision by requiring states to meet quotas for paternity establishment and to improve child support collections.

The Personal Responsibility Act toughens cooperation requirements further by obliging states to punish mothers who do not convince child support agencies that they have told everything they know about their children's fathers. Henceforth, if a mother fails to cooperate to the state's satisfaction, it must reduce her family's grant by at least 25 percent and may deny it altogether.[12]

A mother's cooperation in the establishment of paternity can be a painful and protracted matter: it typically takes fifteen or sixteen months to obtain a paternity order, even when mothers are fully cooperating and the state has all the information it needs to proceed.[13] No longer are mothers rewarded for cooperation in the establishment and enforcement of a child support order, either: the PRA ends the $50 "pass-through," the portion of monthly child support payments which the old welfare law required states to allow mothers to keep.[14] Moreover, while the PRA (like the Family Support Act before it) requires mothers' cooperation in establishing and enforcing child support orders, it does not obligate states to secure payments. In a 1997 decision, the Supreme Court held that child support provisions in welfare law do not give individual mothers rights to force states to meet the terms of the federal law. In other words, a mother who has cooperated with a state agency has no individual claim against that agency if it fails to collect child support payments on her children's behalf.[15]

Regardless of this Catch-22, the paternity establishment and child support provisions compel mothers who receive welfare to pursue absent, derelict, or impoverished fathers, obligating them to assist government's efforts to make those fathers pay support.[16] All fathers who do not pay will be subject to automatic wage withholding and to work requirements.[17] Depending on where he resides, a delinquent father may lose his driver's, occupational, and recreational licenses.[18] If he owes more than $5,000 he may lose his passport.[19] These various measures concede that mothers may live separately from the biological fathers of their children, but insist that they may not live independently of them.

Welfare law thus coerces mothers who are single and poor into relations with fathers. Although the law permits a mother to seek an exception from such relations, it also permits the state to decide whether her reasons are valid and in the best interests of her child. Some mothers will not be able to convince their states that they or their children are victims of violence, let alone endangered by it (perhaps violence is their family secret; perhaps welfare workers find them combative; perhaps they look strong enough to defend themselves and their children). So some poor mothers and children will have to associate with fathers who do not or should not have social connections with their children. The child support requirements not only threaten mothers' and children's safety, they compel mothers to permit association between fathers and children and thereby to jeopardize their own care and custody of children. Further, since legal action for child support often precipitates or exacerbates abuse, they forcibly expose poor mothers to private violence.[20] Paternity establishment requirements, meanwhile, give government power to demand the identity of an unmarried mother's sexual partner, even though her decision not to marry may have been, among other things, a decision not to let government into her most intimate life. (A marriage license creates a presumption of sexual and procreative activities between the named parties.) Giving government the right to know the biological fathers of welfare mothers' children, paternity establishment requirements uniquely injure the privacy rights of poor single mothers who never have been married.

As this chapter will demonstrate, mandatory paternity establishment and child support provisions mark poor single mothers as a separate caste, subject to a separate system of law. The system of law under which they live penalizes their moral choices, prescribes intimate associations that may be unwanted, and infringes rights guarded as fundamental to the personhood of all other citizens. Welfare law thus activates constitutionally significant distinctions among mothers who need welfare and between such mothers and other citizens—distinctions that enforce inequality.

As a first order of inequality, paternity and child support provisions make a poor mother's marital and economic status the measure of her rights. For example, compulsory paternity regulations distinguish non-marital from marital mothers, even if both need welfare. A once-married mother who applies for welfare need not reveal the details of her child's conception to government, even if the man to whom she was married when her child was born is not the biological father, for the law gives the presumption of paternity to the birth mother's husband.[21] Paternity and child support requirements also distinguish among mothers based on economic need. A non-marital mother who does not need welfare has no obligation to name her child's father, and, whether divorced or never-married, a mother who does not need welfare is free not to pursue child support. But a mother who does need cash or medical assistance must permit government to collect child support from whomever government deems to be her child's father (unless

she qualifies for a "good cause" exemption and can convince
her state to grant her one). Failure to cooperate can compromise
a family's welfare eligibility in perpetuity: in 1993, the Supreme
Court let stand a decision that a mother's failure to cooperate
with a welfare agency in establishing paternity and child support for a child born fourteen years earlier made her ineligible
for Medicaid assistance for a new pregnancy.[22]

A comparison of welfare law and paternity law reveals a
second dimension of poor single mothers' distinctive legal status. Welfare law makes the biological connection between men
and children the basis for assigning paternal rights and responsibilities. In contrast, paternity law denies paternal rights and
prerogatives to men who claim them on the basis of biology
alone. Welfare law inflicts family associations on mothers who
need welfare; paternity law defends other mothers against
such association. Welfare law tells a mother who *has to be* her
child's father, while paternity law tells a mother who *gets to be.*

Welfare law subjects poor single mothers to differential treatment in a third respect. Singling out poor single mothers for
inferior legal and constitutional protection, welfare law invades rights that in other contexts are shielded as fundamental:
procreative liberty, marital freedom, and the right to the care
and custody of one's own children. Although none of these
rights is absolute—government may remove a child from the
custody of abusive parents, for example—the Court has concluded that government cannot penalize or burden fundamental rights without providing a compelling justification for doing
so.[23] Moreover, the Court has maintained since 1963 that if
government cannot take away fundamental rights directly, it
cannot do so indirectly by requiring individuals to forfeit their
rights in exchange for subsistence.[24] Yet under welfare law,
government tells needy mothers of non-marital children to
yield sexual privacy—to divulge the information it says it re-

quires to establish paternity (with whom have you had sex? how often? where? did you practice birth control?).[25] In exchange for benefits, mothers must sacrifice decisional autonomy about family relationships, leaving it to states to decide whether to exempt abused mothers from child support requirements and to determine whether abuse has taken place (were you drunk or on drugs? did you provoke him? did you call the police?). Ultimately mothers must cede independence as persons and as parents, for they are forced into relations of economic dependence with biological fathers who then may claim rights to custody and visitation.

These effects of paternity-based child support enforcement in welfare law will not injure all, or perhaps even most, poor single mothers who need welfare. Most mothers know the identity of their children's fathers and many want them to contribute to the support of their children.[26] The point is not the body count but the stratification of rights; not how many mothers are harmed but that *any* might be by the conditioning of mothers' citizenship rights on means and marital status.


## Making Mothers Pay

In September 1993, an article in the conservative *American Enterprise* observed, "Many people support the unwed mother's right to decide how much contact she wants to have with her baby's father, and therefore her right not to name him. . . . Policy toward unwed fathers is being pulled in two opposite directions. Both are likely to be resisted by those whose primary interest is in the well-being and autonomy of the mother."[27] But in the rounds of debate that culminated in the enactment of the Personal Responsibility Act of 1996, no policymaker examined the consequences to mothers of heightened paternal obligations; no policymaker expressed "primary interest" in the autonomy of mothers. In a disturbing trend, instead of firing rejoinders at conservatives, liberals parroted them. William Galston, a domestic policy advisor to President Clinton, long has bemoaned divorce and non-marital child-birth: "Sharply rising rates of divorce, unwed mothers, and runaway fathers represent abuses of individual freedom, for they are patterns of adult behavior with profoundly negative effects on children."[28] William Julius Wilson, another intellec-tual with the ear of President Clinton, long has promoted mar-riage as a solution to poverty among African Americans in the inner cities.[29] In testimony before the House Ways and Means Committee, Donna Shalala, secretary of Health and Human Services, defied "anyone in public life . . . to condone children born out of wedlock."[30] Congresswomen, including feminists Barbara Kennelly (D-Connecticut), Patricia Schroeder (D-Colorado), and Lynn Woolsey (D-California), pushed legisla-tion cracking down on "deadbeat dads," calling stringent child support enforcement an alternative to welfare.[31]

The Personal Responsibility Act codifies the claim that mar-riage is the best antipoverty policy. The insistence on a family economy in which fathers pay for children that women raise is not some detritus from prefeminist welfare politics. Rather, it represents a working consensus among conservatives, moder-ates, and liberals—including many middle-class feminists—that a return to paternal responsibility will diminish the need for welfare. Indeed, across thirty years of welfare reform, the only true faith has been in the child support obligation of the absent father.[32] With Republicans and Democrats—including feminists in both parties—in agreement on this score, it is no wonder that the PRA makes marriage and its economic surrogate (child support) both the means to and the ends of welfare reform.

Liberals, conservatives, and middle-class feminists all insist that fathers have a central role to play in alleviating or ending poor single mothers' need for welfare, but they argue from very different starting points. Religious conservatives are eager to enforce heterosexual marriage, whatever the context, simply because it is holy. Other conservatives take a more instrumental tack to the same moral conclusion, stressing the salubrious moral effects of fathers on children, rather than the economic costs of fathers' unmet obligations to them. David Blankenhorn, the founder and president of the Institute for American Values, contends that fathers have a "distinctive capacity to contribute to the identity, character, and competence of [their] children."[33] The sociologist David Popenoe underscores fathers' "vital role . . . in promoting cooperation and other . . . virtues: . . . fathers, it turns out, may be of special importance for the development of [empathy], essential to an ordered society of law-abiding, cooperative, and compassionate adults."[34]

Conservatives such as George Gilder are less concerned with the effects of fathers on children than with the necessity of father-headed family life for social order.[35] Perhaps the most extreme—and most influential—version of these views came from Charles Murray. As he wrote in his 1993 clarion call to end welfare, "Illegitimacy is the single most important social problem of our time—more important than crime, drugs, poverty, illiteracy, welfare or homelessness because it drives everything else."[36] Following Murray's cue, conservatives in Congress pledged to promote father-mother families by penalizing non-marital mothers who remain incorrigibly single.[37] H.R. 4, the original Republican welfare bill, would have made good on this promise, denying cash assistance to children born to mothers on welfare (the family cap) and disqualifying unmarried teenage mothers from welfare altogether. Echoing Murray, House

Republican whip Tom Delay (R-Texas) reasoned that welfare "encourages violence, predatory sex, total anarchy within that community. It has created a whole culture of dependent people that is destroying the fabric of families . . . mostly in the inner cities."[38]

Some liberals likewise connect single parenting to social disorder and promote marriage as the optimal structure of roles and relationships within which to raise morally fit children. Policy scholar and Democratic senator Daniel Patrick Moynihan, for example, connects fatherless families to "crime, violence, unrest, unrestrained lashing out at the whole social structure."[39] Others stress the fiscal benefits of marriage: noting that women and children make up 80 percent of the poverty population and that 53 percent of mother-only families are poor, they argue that the two-parent family protects the public treasury, since families headed by fathers generally do not need cash assistance from government to survive.[40] Emphasizing child welfare, still other liberals find children in father-mother families to be better off—less poor, more protected—than children in mother-only families.[41] These assessments lead some liberals to join conservatives such as Murray who view single mothers as having caused their own poverty by choosing to exit or eschew marriage. Other liberals blame the poverty of mother-only families on deadbeat dads.[42] Whether to save the government money (by some accounts, if all eligible children had support orders and all designated parents fully paid them, some $46 billion could be collected[43]) or to improve the economic lot of children, liberals have been especially vigorous proponents of aggressive child support enforcement.

Feminists complete this odd consensus for paternal responsibility with their own broad calls for more effective child support enforcement. Less likely than male policymakers to sing fathers' virtues because they belong to fathers, or to demand marriage because it is moral, feminists have been drawn into the consensus through the logic of fathers' responsibilities, especially their financial responsibilities to support their children. The issue for feminists has not been the unique value of fathers as mates or care-givers, but the unique costs of their desertion, as income providers for mothers and their children.

Finding the costs of childbearing that fall disproportionately on women a main source of gender inequality, many feminists want men to provide for their biological children even if they have no relationship with them.[44] In the welfare context, many feminists see poverty as the first among inequalities that follow from mothers' care-giving obligations. Hence the essayist Katha Pollitt once argued, in a review of the welfare debate, that "fair's fair. . . . A man who fathers a child out of wedlock must pay $10,000 a year or 20 percent of his income, whichever is greater, in child support until the child reaches 21."[45] The idea that biological paternity establishes a man's obligation to children supports the contention that if biological fathers would meet their responsibilities, poor single mothers wouldn't have to turn to welfare. Middle-class feminists thus turn on its head the famous lament attributed to welfare rights activist Johnnie Tillmon. Whereas Tillmon long ago complained that AFDC mothers traded in *a* man for *the* man, many middle-class feminists today call upon welfare mothers to trade in *the* man for *sperm* man.

Feminists in Congress have been particularly emphatic about resolving the child support crisis through increased federal involvement in the enforcement of support orders, especially across state lines. In fact, without their interventions, especially in the House of Representatives, paternity-based child support would not be the major pillar of the new welfare policy that it has become. The first version of H.R. 4, introduced into the new Republican Congress in January 1995, spoke only of paternity establishment for non-marital children and not at all about enforcing economic obligations of non-marital fathers—primarily because the Republicans' goal was not to devise an economic surrogate for marriage (child support) but to enforce marriage itself. Feminist congresswomen who had sponsored model child support enforcement legislation in the previous Congress berated Republicans for their omission.[46] Embarrassed, Republican leaders adopted the Democrats' child support enforcement provisions as their own.

Although the "deadbeat dad" thesis has been popular among middle-class feminists in recent years, they have not always embraced welfare law's paternity and child support provisions unequivocally. At the 1974 child support hearings, for example, representatives of the National Organization for Women expressed some reservations about the compulsory nature of the paternity establishment proposal while congratulating Congress for making child support enforcement a federal matter. Meanwhile, the League of Women Voters announced its opposition to the child support bill, arguing that its coercive discrimination against poor mothers overrode any potential benefits from increased child support collection.[47]

Still, the goal of "making fathers pay" appealed widely among feminists by the 1980s. Many were key players in the child support enforcement debate of the early 1980s, with Congresswoman Barbara Kennelly sponsoring legislation to strengthen enforcement and women's groups working successfully for its passage in 1984.[48] As momentum for more aggressive enforcement against fathers grew, opposition to the coercion of mothers dimmed. By the 1990s, middle-class feminist outrage against deadbeat dads drowned out objections to mandatory maternal cooperation in the establishment of paternity and child support. During the first years of the Clinton administration, many feminists pressed for enhanced paternity-based child support enforcement as a means to reform welfare, arguing that irresponsible fathers, not immoral mothers, were the cause of maternal and child poverty. Some feminists participated in official policy discussions: representatives from groups such as the National Women's Law Center and the Women's Legal Defense Fund, for example, participated in the development of the child support provisions of the Clinton welfare bill, which were later incorporated into the Personal Responsibility Act.[49]

Incautious pursuit of rigorous child support enforcement aligned middle-class feminists behind a coercive policy that actually endangers the rights of poor single mothers. Setting them apart from other mothers, coerced maternal cooperation in the establishment of paternity and child support harms poor single mothers alone. Simultaneously answering patriarchal anxieties about paternity and feminist frustrations over child support, paternity-based child support provisions beef up services that deserted middle-class mothers may choose to employ, but that are imposed on poor single mothers.

The gender system that renders women vulnerable to inequality in both private and public life pivots on the patriarchal family. So it should be deeply troubling to feminists that welfare reform makes responsible fathers the solution to maternal and child poverty. But many feminists don't see it that way and fail to appreciate the reactionary thrust of the paternity and child support provisions of welfare law. Perhaps to some, paternity and child support have been elements of welfare policy for so long that they are no longer controversial despite their patriarchal implications. More likely, child support is such a hot-button issue for middle-class women and feminists that they have been blinded to the distinction between child support that is sought and child support that is imposed. Feminists in Congress did author free-standing child support enforcement bills that focused on fathers irrespective of mothers' need for welfare,[50] but they also conflated child support enforcement with welfare reform.

No doubt, middle-class feminist energy behind stringent paternity establishment and child support enforcement is animated in part by exasperation with some men's cost-free exploitation of the sexual revolution. From this perspective, men ought to be held responsible for the procreative consequences of their heightened access to women's bodies. The quest for fairness in procreative relations drives the increasingly punitive proposals (such as seizing of bank accounts and pension funds) designed to force fathers to meet their obligations to children. But middle-class feminists' frustration with irresponsible fathers doesn't explain their willingness to compel cooperation from mothers.

Perhaps the explanation is that when middle-class women think of the circumstances that might lead them to welfare, they think of divorce—from middle-class men who then refuse to chip in for the care and maintenance of children. Congresswoman Lynn Woolsey (D-California) is a case in point. Something of a Beltway icon during the welfare debate, she described herself and was described by other opponents of Republican welfare reform as "a typical welfare mother." Thirty years earlier, she had had to turn to welfare following her divorce from a man she describes as "very successful."[51] Though she had a support order, she "never received a penny in child support."[52] Woolsey's story provided a useful strategic intervention into the welfare debate, countering the stereotypic image of welfare mothers as Black and unmarried. But marking one mother's story, however uplifting, as representative of a whole population invites the kind of solipsism that produces one-size-fits-all policy prescriptions. Such prescriptions are not only unworkable, they also neglect the needs of people with different life stories and often threaten their rights.

The compulsory features of paternity establishment and child support enforcement may be unremarkable to a divorced mother with a support order: she escapes compulsion by choosing to pursue child support, and what matters to her is that the support order be enforced. But some mothers do not have support orders because they do not want them. They do not want to identify fathers; or do not want fathers involved with children; or do not want to expose fathers to harsh penalties when they cannot pay what a court tells them they owe. For many poor mothers, child support orders against poor fathers are also not worth the risk of violence. Poor mothers know, moreover, that child support is not an alternative to welfare where fathers are themselves poor: in 1989, the average annual child support award for poor mothers was only $1,889.[53] As one analyst put it, for poor fathers "child support collection has turned into an income transfer program [for] lawyers and welfare bureaucrats."[54] Mothers also know that the threat of a support order can discourage fathers whose only resource is emotional from participating at all in the lives of their children.

"Making fathers pay" may promote the economic and justice interests of many custodial mothers. But *making mothers* make fathers pay means trading their rights and safety for subsistence. The issue is not whether government should assist mothers in collecting payments from fathers. Of course it should. Neither is the issue whether child support enforcement provisions in welfare policy help mothers who have or desire child support awards. Of course they do. Nor is the issue whether it is a good thing for children to have active fathers. Of course it can be. The issue is coercion of mothers who have eschewed patriarchal conventions (whether by choice or from necessity). The issue is also coercion directed toward mothers whose deviation from patriarchal norms has been associated with their racial and cultural standing.

Paternity establishment and child support became strategies for welfare reform not because of the unjust effects of divorce on mothers but because of the allegedly unsavory behavior of mothers of non-marital children. It is non-marital childbearing, not divorce, that has been blamed for social pathologies like crime and dependency. The preamble to the Personal Responsibility Act legislates precisely this point of view. Such patriarchal reasoning slides into racial argument, as the discourse of welfare reform specifically correlates non-marital childbearing rates among African Americans with social and moral decay.[55]

Divorce or separation more often triggers initial welfare use than does non-marital childbearing. But as welfare foes like to point out, 47.5 percent of welfare mothers in 1993 had never been married—as compared to 22.7 percent who were widowed or divorced, 17.3 percent who were married but whose husbands were absent, and 12.6 percent who were married and living with husbands.[56] Further, 68 percent of mothers receiving welfare were not married at the time of their first child's birth.[57] Opponents of welfare cite these data as evidence linking welfare to immorality. They follow with the fact that welfare participation rates among women of color have been disproportionate to their percentage of the population (though commensurate with the racial distribution of poverty) to implant race in the nexus of welfare and immorality.[58] The fact that only 28.4 percent of non-marital mothers receiving welfare are white further excites this racialized welfare politics, focusing attention on "those people" who are in need of reform.[59] Not surprisingly, the core tropes of antiwelfare politics have tied "illegitimacy" and "welfare dependency" to Black unmarried motherhood. Taken as a whole, welfare law aims to reform all poor single mothers. But the faces summoned by welfare discourse are Black—welfare "queens" whose character is judged wanting.

The racialized gender politics of welfare have yielded reforms that subordinate women of color disproportionately, both ideologically and in their practical effects. Poor women of color suffer stigmas applied only to them (lazy, matriarchal, baby machines). They also have unique needs for welfare: less likely to begin a welfare spell because of divorce than white women, women of color are also more likely to be connected to poor men. Hence, although paternity-based child support ultimately erodes the rights of all poor single mothers, the policy injures women of color particularly and directly. The product of racism, patriarchalism, and solipsism, the new law hardens inequalities among women.

## Paternity Law and Welfare Law

Thirty years ago, biological paternity did not automatically incur a legally enforceable child support obligation. Paternity law still does not derive fatherhood from mere biology except when mothers seek to establish paternity. But when non-marital mothers and children need welfare, welfare law assigns obligations to biological fathers regardless of mothers' and children's desires. Paternity law and welfare law thus ascribe starkly different meanings to biological paternity and subject fathers and mothers to very different relationships in the family and with the state, depending on marital status and on economic need.

Paternity law and welfare law began to diverge sharply in 1973. In that year, Congress held hearings on a child support bill that soon became law. The purpose of the Child Support

Act of 1974, in the words of proponent Senator Russell Long, was to "make papa pay" and thereby remove alleged incentives to non-marital childbearing and child-raising among women who received welfare. At the heart of child support policy is the assumption that biological fathers bear financial responsibility for non-marital mothers' children, whether or not biological fathers have relationships with them. By assigning legal paternity and financial responsibility to fathers on the basis of biology alone, welfare law confers on biological fathers the legal status of parent.

In 1973 also, congressional proponents of vigorous child support enforcement against non-marital fathers received a boost from the Supreme Court. In *Gomez v. Perez,* the Court ruled that if a state grants marital children a statutory right to paternal support, it must also do so for non-marital children. As a result, all states now have paternity laws under which a non-marital father can be compelled to support his children if the children and their mother wish him to do so. These statutes, however, do not compel mothers and children to seek paternal support.

Again in 1973, the National Conference of Commissioners on Uniform State Laws promulgated the Uniform Parentage Act, which established a presumption of legitimacy, or marital presumption of paternity, for all children conceived during and born into marriages. The marital presumption means that for the purposes of legal paternity it is irrelevant whether the child of a married mother who cohabits with her husband was actually biologically fathered by a man other than the mother's husband. Not all states officially adopted the Uniform Parentage Act, but most states enforce its marital presumption. Thus, at least in the context of marriage, it is the family relationship, rather than sperm, that determines the rights and obligations of fatherhood.[60]

Paternity law pivots on marriage. But it constrains the rights of sperm outside of marriage, as well. As vetted by the Supreme Court, paternity law holds that a mere biological connection does not automatically confer legal paternity and parental rights on a non-marital biological father, even when the mother of his child was not married to someone else at the time of his child's birth. The Supreme Court has examined this issue on several occasions since the mid-1970s, each time refusing to find a fundamental right to a parental relationship based on biological paternity alone.[61] Although the Court has not spelled out a definitive paternity doctrine, it has consistently reasoned that absent a "substantial relationship" between a non-marital biological father and his child, the "mere existence of a biological link does not merit . . . constitutional protection."[62] Arguing that the rights of a mother and a father may well be different depending on the relationship of each to the child, the Court defined biological paternity as an opportunity rather than a legal status: "The significance of the biological connection is that it offers the natural father an opportunity that no other male possesses to develop a relationship with his offspring. If he grasps that opportunity and accepts some measure of responsibility for the child's future, he may enjoy the blessings of the parent-child relationship. . . . If he fails to do so, the Federal Constitution will not automatically compel a state to listen to his opinion of where the child's best interests lie."[63]

Even if a non-marital biological father can demonstrate a substantial relationship with his child—that is, show that he provided financial support or gave care—his paternal rights are not protected absolutely. The Court holds the marital presumption paramount even where the non-marital biological father has lived with, supported, and cared for his child.[64] In *Michael H. v. Gerald D.*, the Court defended the parental rights of a marital mother's husband even though the mother conceived her child with another man and was estranged from her husband for some time after the child's birth. In the Court's view, the biological father's claim to paternity jeopardized the integrity of the marital family, for from paternity flow rights: "If Michael were successful in being declared the father, other rights would follow—most importantly, the right to be considered as the parent who should have custody . . . a status which 'embrace[s] the sum of parental rights with respect to the rearing of a child, including the child's care . . . the right to make decisions regarding the control, education, and health of the child . . . and the right, as well as the duty, to prepare the child for additional obligations, which includes the teaching of moral standards, religious beliefs, and elements of good citizenship.'"[65]

In championing the role of the marital patriarch, *Michael H.* does not disturb the gender conventions that subject women to inequality in the family. But it and the paternity law it affirms does offer mothers some choices about what kinds of relationships to foster between non-marital fathers and their children—indeed, whether to foster any at all. Most important, paternity law permits mothers to resist the claims of non-marital fathers to parental rights based solely on biology. Welfare law, by contrast, insists that non-marital mothers honor fathers' biological connection to children. It requires non-marital welfare mothers to permit biological fathers to develop the very "substantial relationships" with children that paternity law holds are *prerequisite* to paternal rights.

Where the marital presumption is not at issue, paternity law measures the non-marital father–child relationship by the amount and quality of time father and child spend together, as well as by the degree and regularity of financial support tendered. Paternity law requires a father to take initiative in building a relationship with his child. Welfare law substitutes coercion for this burden of volition, literally forcing non-marital fathers to meet paternity law's test of a "substantial relationship." The child support provision does this by requiring the establishment and modification of each father's economic obligation, then by enforcing that obligation with work requirements and various other penalties for deadbeat dads.[66] The provision also gives incentives to states to cultivate and enforce fathers' access to and visitation with children. States may seek federal grants specifically to facilitate connections between noncustodial parents (fathers) and children, grants which may be spent to compel custodial mothers who receive welfare into mediation with fathers about visitation and custody arrangements.[67]

These various stipulations of the Personal Responsibility Act subject all welfare fathers to a police state, where they are subject to liens, withholding of wages, credit investigations, and exposure to employers, among other sanctions. They further indenture poor fathers (as well as irresponsible ones) in work programs ordered by courts and state agencies. This policy medicine has been on the table for quite some time. A dozen years ago, Daniel Patrick Moynihan urged such muscular enforcement of biological fathers' responsibility: "The absent father is rarely really absent, especially the teenage father, but merely unwilling or not required to acknowledge his children's presence. . . . [F]or the too-much-pitied unemployed teenage male there would be nothing wrong with a federal work program—compulsory when a court has previously ordered him to support his children—with the wages shared between father and mother."[68]

Equally important, child support policy mandates that poor mothers must participate in their own undoing as custodial mothers. As I have suggested above, coercing mothers to cooperate in child support enforcement amounts to coercing them to make it possible for welfare fathers to acquire parental rights: at the very least, the legal designation of paternity entitles fathers to claim visitation with children. In other words, as a condition of receiving welfare, mothers must put their very parenthood at risk. This is not a fictive risk: a common tactic used by non-custodial parents in child support cases is to counterclaim for custody or increased visitation. Worse, some fathers' rights groups have argued before Congress that a mother's application for welfare should in and of itself establish a father's claim to custody, and that welfare law's child support provisions should criminalize a mother's interference with visitation by fathers.[69] Clearly, welfare law creates serious legal problems for poor single mothers—without providing legal assistance to fight them.[70] A mother's only alternative to an expensive legal battle against the man whom welfare law designates as her child's father is to marry another man.[71]

Child support policy invades the rights of both marital and non-marital welfare mothers just because they are poor. But paternity establishment policy threatens the parental rights of non-marital welfare mothers uniquely and severely. Recall the Supreme Court's caution in *Michael H.*: "If Michael were successful in being declared the father, *other rights would follow— most importantly, the right to be considered as the parent who should have custody*" (emphasis added). The paternity establishment condition of welfare eligibility requires a non-marital mother to disclose the identity of her child's father at the cost of community censure, the cost of her family's preference, and even the cost of her safety. Although the Court elsewhere has found it "unreasonable" for government to expect a non-marital mother swiftly to divulge her child's paternity—has guessed that it might, in fact, be *years* before she could comfortably do so—welfare law has spurned this doctrine.[72] Illegitimacy law and paternity law have alleviated discriminations against non-marital children and have balanced the biology-based claims of non-marital fathers against the relational rights of mothers. Welfare law, by contrast, is intent on returning non-marital mothers and children to the father-headed family—if not in legal form, at least in economic fact.

## Rights at Risk

Paternity establishment and child support requirements serve the new statutory purposes of welfare law, which are to reduce non-marital births and promote the two-parent family. To accomplish these ends, welfare law wields some pretty big sticks: most important, it obliges poor single mothers to exchange fundamental rights for subsistence.

One of these rights is family privacy—the right of individuals to decide their own family affairs, including, presumably, their own family's structure. The Supreme Court has defended such rights strictly for seventy-five years. Beginning with *Meyer v. Nebraska* in 1923, the Court has consistently honored "the rights to conceive and to raise one's children" as essential rights.[73] Asserting that "it is cardinal with us that the custody, care and nurture of the child reside first in the parents,"[74] the Court has accorded special constitutional protection to choices about family living and custodial arrangements,[75] to relational rights of parents and children,[76] and to parents' child-rearing decisions.[77] The Court reaffirmed the fundamental nature of family rights in 1996, in a case involving the termination of a mother's parental rights: "Choices about marriage, family life, and the upbringing of children are among associational rights . . . recognized as 'of basic importance in our society.'"[78] Government cannot intrude upon choices the Court has deemed of "vital personal interest" without powerful—and constitutional—justification to do so. Yet welfare law directly interferes with poor single mothers' decisions about child-rearing and family life by compelling them to establish legal relations between children and fathers.

Among the associational rights infringed by welfare law is the freedom to marry, or not marry. A host of cases establishes that "marriage is one of the 'basic civil rights of man,' fundamental to our very existence and survival."[79] The landmark decision *Loving v. Virginia*, which struck down antimiscegenation laws, specifically included the right to *not* marry as among the marital freedoms the Constitution protects. In *United States v. Kras* the Court clarified its reasoning, recalling that on "many occasions we have recognized the fundamental importance . . . under our Constitution . . . of the associational interests that surround the establishment and dissolution of the marital relationship."[80] Applying the strict constitutional tests necessary to protect fundamental liberties, the Court in *Zablocki v. Redhail* further reasoned that marital rights could not be conditioned on the economic status or economic obligations of the parties involved.[81] While welfare law does not govern marital decisions directly, it impairs marital freedom by subjecting mothers who are not married to coerced paternity establishment and child support enforcement, two measures intended to simulate the marital family economy.

Welfare law also infringes the sexual and reproductive privacy rights of non-marital mothers, rights which the Court began to establish thirty-two years ago when it barred government from the (heterosexual) bedroom. Locating the right to "the marital relation and the marital home" in the fundamental right to privacy, the Court in *Griswold v. Connecticut* shielded married couples from governmental intrusion into contraceptive decisions.[82] The Court extended the guarantee of contraceptive privacy to single adults in 1972, holding that "if the right of privacy means anything, it is the right of the *individual,* married or single, to be free from unwarranted governmental intrusion into matters so fundamentally affecting a person as the decision whether to bear or beget a child."[83] *Roe v. Wade* applied this reasoning to a woman's decision to continue or terminate a pregnancy, thereby recognizing a fundamental constitutional right to reproductive choice.[84] Welfare law interferes with poor unmarried mothers' reproductive lives by imposing punishment (coerced paternity establishment and child support, as well as the family cap) when they exercise the wrong reproductive choice.[85]

In these various ways, welfare law diminishes the citizenship of all poor single mothers who need governmental assistance to survive, reserving its most draconian prescriptions for poor mothers of non-marital children. Although the new time limits make welfare assistance temporary, the exchange of rights for assistance can have permanent effects: on the safety and survival of mothers and children, on the integrity of family decisions, and on the procreative personhood of women.

These invasions of rights are not merely theoretical. They are real, and their effects are irreparable. Consider the mother whose first child was conceived in a gang rape thirteen years ago. When she applied for welfare in Virginia in February 1996, she was told that she had to name her daughter's father. Although she had put the rape behind her, she had to retell it to her caseworker. Even so, since she neither knew the names of her stranger assailants nor reported the incident to the police at the time, she could neither establish paternity nor win a good cause exemption. Her benefits were cut.[86]

Or consider Minerva, compelled by her welfare agency to upset her baby daughter's relations with her biological father in a paternity action against him. Not only did she have to jeopardize delicate and voluntary family relations by acceding to government coercion, she also had to disclose intimate details in an open courtroom. Who is the baby's father? When did you first have sex with him? How often? When did you last have sex with him? When did you last have sex with him before your last period? Did you have sex with anyone else?[87]

Rita Roe also had to provide information about her child's biological father, including his name, address, and social security number, as well as the make, model, and license number of his car. Eighteen-year-old Rita was mildly retarded and had been impregnated by a drifter. Under the mandatory maternal cooperation provision, Rita was required to confess to the state that she didn't know much about her child's father. Although she cooperated in the state's invasion of her privacy, her inability to provide the required details resulted in a loss of benefits, including provisions for child care.[88]

And then there's Joy Tomas, who swore to her caseworker that she did not know who fathered her child. Joy had conceived her child through casual sex on Waikiki Beach with a stranger known only as "Boy." In this case, welfare law required a non-marital mother to reveal to the government her participation in activities that society harshly rebukes. But she did attest to such activities and to her resulting inability to establish her child's paternity. Nevertheless, the welfare agency declared this lack of knowledge a "failure to cooperate" and accordingly withheld welfare benefits. Despite the consistency of her story across numerous retellings, the welfare agency would not restore her benefits.[89]

Or what about my student Jane Smith? When she became pregnant accidentally by her then-boyfriend, Bill, their relationship soured. He wanted her to terminate the pregnancy, but she wanted to have the child. They went their separate ways, with Jane deciding that Bill should not be obligated to the child in any way, since it was her decision to become a mother. Meeting the demands of an infant made it too taxing to stay in school. The expense of child care made it unaffordable to get a full-time job, which is what she needed to get by. So Jane applied for welfare, thinking it would help her return to school or get some job training, or maybe even find a part-time job. But she was turned away when she would not identify her child's father and help establish a support order against him.

In all five women's experiences, rights that are fundamental to women's liberty and equality succumbed to welfare stipulations. Even under the old welfare law, poor mothers' rights fell before government's interest in making mothers economically dependent on fathers. Paternity establishment and child support requirements long have put government on the side of inequality, where it not only treated poor mothers differently from other mothers and childless women, but where it also cultivated unequal relations of gender power in the family. The Personal Responsibility Act deepens this inequality.

And the PRA goes a step further. Until now, federal welfare law was formally neutral on the question of whether poor women have a right to become mothers. To be sure, welfare administrators for several decades used poor women's need for cash or medical assistance as opportunities to control their fertility. From the 1930s into the 1970s, for example, state and local welfare agencies and public hospitals—especially in Puerto Rico, the South, and parts of the Southwest—often terminated poor women's reproductive choices by sterilizing them involuntarily. Invasions of procreative liberty did not stop with mothers: in Alabama, for example, officials forced an illiterate welfare recipient to agree to the sterilization of her young daughters by threatening to cut off benefits. The National Welfare Rights Organization and aggrieved recipients challenged these actions, winning from courts and in federal regulations poor women's right to procreate.[90] Even so, welfare remained linked to fertility in the public—and state legislators'—imagination. In 1990, the *Philadelphia Inquirer* ignited public debate about contraceptive incentives for welfare recipients in an article arguing that one way to reduce poverty is to reduce births to poor women.[91] In 1991 and 1992, some twenty bills were introduced into thirteen state legislatures to induce women on welfare to use Norplant; two of those bills promised bonus payments to welfare recipients who accepted free contraceptive implants.[92] Meanwhile, both the Bush and Clinton administrations gave interested states permission to withhold cash benefits from children born to mothers on welfare. As a matter of law, however, federal welfare statutes before 1996 did not invite, require, or condone such assaults on women's bodies, and federal family planning policy required that family planning services—including sterilization—be voluntarily requested. Official national welfare policy still does not require states to control the fertility of welfare recipients, but it invites states to do so by providing them incentives to reduce and authority to punish non-marital births.

Although Republicans did not succeed in directly sanctioning non-marital births, they did successfully replace the means test for welfare with a means-and-morals test that assesses the legitimacy of poor mothers' economic need in terms of the marital conditions under which they bore their children. So far, nineteen states have stated their intention to implement the family cap under the PRA, thereby sanctioning women who bear a child while poor enough to need welfare. Alongside the family cap, provisions for abstinence education, improved illegitimacy ratios, and supervised teenage motherhood subject poor mothers to separate and unequal laws which can only be escaped by moral redemption to the satisfaction of government. Backed up by mandatory paternity establishment and child support enforcement, these provisions impose penalties on poor mothers who fail moral redemption, penalties that decide who is appropriate to bear children.

The PRA upends reproductive law, which, while protecting women's right not to become mothers, has officially favored women's choice to do so.[93] Thus the Supreme Court has upheld the Hyde Amendment's prohibition against Medicaid funding for abortion, reasoning that while women have the right to make their own reproductive decisions, government has the right to express its reproductive opinions, including a preference for childbirth. Feminists have been most unhappy with the Hyde Amendment because it obstructs poor women's right to avoid pregnancy. But antiabortion Medicaid policy at least has the inadvertent virtue of protecting poor women's choice to bear children against eugenic intervention by the government. In contrast, the PRA creates new opportunities for governmental control of poor women's fertility and strongly states governmental disdain for non-marital motherhood among poor women. Middle-class feminist preoccupation with abortion rights over the years has diverted attention from the range of political demands we must make to fully enjoy reproductive rights in all their dimensions. Now that social supports for poor women who choose motherhood have been repealed, further feminist pursuit of abortion funding for poor women may win policies that encourage them not to bear children—without affirming their right to do so.

The new welfare law is riddled with such dangers. It may lead fathers to claim abortion rights for themselves; if they have to pay for children just because the children bear their DNA, shouldn't they get to decide whether children should be born? It may lead states to require contraceptive use by mothers in exchange for welfare; what better way to reduce both the "illegitimacy ratio" and the abortion rate than by preventing conception? Moreover, it may lead poor women to conclude that they have no choice but to terminate a non-marital pregnancy. The PRA's section on abstinence education requires participating states to teach girls and women who are "most likely to bear children out-of-wedlock" that sex before economic self-sufficiency is wrong.[94] If government can teach women that motherhood belongs only to her who can afford it, why not teach them that if they are poor and pregnant, abortion is their only rational choice?

The new welfare law's explicit stipulations and implicit dangers make it the first national policy since the discredited *Buck v. Bell* decision[95] to officially *disfavor* a woman's choice to become a mother if she is poor and not married at the time of the child's birth. Carrie Buck was a non-marital child who herself became pregnant outside of marriage when she was raped by one of her foster relatives. The state of Virginia institutionalized her to conceal her pregnancy, declared her "feebleminded," and subjected her to compulsory sterilization.[96] In *Buck v. Bell*, Oliver Wendell Holmes defended Virginia's policy of compulsory sterilization for the "feebleminded" on the grounds that "three generations of imbeciles is enough." In the Personal Responsibility Act, Congress declared that one act of immorality is enough. In the PRA, Congress nationalized the eugenic reasoning behind Virginia's 1924 sterilization policy: "many defective persons . . . if incapable of procreating, might be discharged with safety and become self-supporting with benefit to themselves and to society."[97] In other words, poor women may well be productive citizens, but only so long as they are not reproductive citizens—only so long as they are not mothers.[98]

The welfare debate revealed that except among the purest of abortion foes, the fact of illegitimacy is more morally freighted than the act of abortion; the need to teach "those people" not to reproduce unless they can afford it is more urgent than the call to protect the unborn; and the demand to reform welfare is more righteous than the struggle to preserve life. As conservative values entrepreneur William Kristol phrased it, "we can't not reform welfare because it might lead to a few more abortions."[99] And so welfare law now officially requires or permits states to discourage births among poor women without husbands, by restricting the rights and undermining the survival of women who flout the new law's moral strictures.

# 4

## Why Should Poor Single Mothers Have
## to Work Outside the Home?

### Work Requirements and the Negation of Mothers

**M**ore intrusive and patriarchal than any national welfare policy we've ever known, the Personal Responsibility Act tells the poor single mother that if she doesn't participate in a father-mother family, she surrenders her right to care for her children. Although outside work can especially compromise a poor mother's ability to attend to her children's schedule and range of needs, the PRA makes it the paramount requirement for poor mothers who are persistently single. In impairing their capacity to meet their personal responsibilities as parents, the PRA thus repudiates them as mothers.

We have been inching inexorably toward this outcome for thirty years. Moving steadily rightward since 1967, welfare reformers have asserted with increasing militancy that welfare harms poor families, ruins moral values, destroys initiative, and saps independence. Accordingly, they amended the Aid to Families with Dependent Children program numerous times across the decades, slowly embedding in welfare law the expectation that poor single mothers seek self-sufficiency in the labor market. The Personal Responsibility Act turns this expectation into a legal obligation.

The PRA's work provisions begin by requiring solo care-givers who have received benefits for two months to perform community service work with hours and tasks fixed by the states.[1] For solo care-givers who have accumulated twenty-four (consecutive or nonconsecutive) months on welfare, the PRA stiffens work rules, requiring increasing hours of work outside the home: twenty hours in 1998, thirty hours in 2000 and thereafter. The law backs up its requirement for individuals with a requirement for states: each state must enroll an annually increasing percentage of its caseload (30 percent in 1998, fifty percent in 2002 and thereafter) in "work activities."[2] If a recipient does not undertake some approved form of re-munerated or unremunerated outside work, her state must ei-ther reduce or terminate her family's benefits.[3] If a state does not satisfy mandated work participation rates, it loses a per-centage of its block grant.[4] Because states must enroll fifty per-cent of their caseloads in work outside the home by 2002, ever larger numbers of recipients will have to seek employment immediately upon receiving benefits. The coup de grace in the PRA's work program is its five-year lifetime limit for adult welfare participation, which the law permits states to restrict even further. The drop-dead time limit forces the poor single mother either to work outside the home or to enter into private association with someone who will provide economically for her and her children.

The Act does permit some exceptions to mandatory work by single mothers. Although the law requires community service work by recipients after two months on welfare, for example, it allows states to opt out of this requirement by letter to the Secretary of Health and Human Services.[5] Also, though work requirements are mandatory for single mothers, states have the option to exempt single mothers with children younger than age one.[6] These exceptions will relax work requirements for some single mothers, yet only if states choose to allow them.

**105**

Why Should Poor Single Mothers Have to Work Outside the Home?

The Act also requires states to ease work requirements where child care is unavailable. A state must continue assistance to a mother whose child is under six years of age if she can prove to the state's satisfaction that she cannot secure suitable informal child care from a relative or friend, or "appropriate and afford-able" formal care within a reasonable distance from her home or workplace.[7] This exception will assist some mothers, yet its language is so open-ended that states retain considerable discretion to decide the "suitability" of informal arrangements, decide who is a relative, decide what kind of formal care is "appropriate and affordable," and decide what is a "reasonable distance" from home or work.

While the PRA's work requirements may not be hermetic, they are exacting and difficult to escape. Gone are the equivoca-tions about compelling single mothers to work outside the home, which marked welfare policy to one degree or another ever since the Work Incentive Program was created in 1967.[8] Throwing the full weight of welfare law behind market labor by poor single mothers, the PRA ends welfare by redefining it. Economic provision for mothers' care of children was once the primary purpose of welfare. Now, welfare law scorns care-giving by poor single mothers and so spurns their children. Moreover, it makes the moral regulation of mothers welfare's principal objective.

Work requirements are a crucial lever in this moral regula-tion, as they make life more difficult for mothers who are par-enting alone. Furthermore, they explicitly reward marriage: mothers who fulfill the law's purpose of "encourag[ing] the formation and maintenance of two-parent families"[9] do not have to work outside the home, even if their families continue to need welfare. Unless the family receives federally funded child care assistance—unlikely, should the mother choose to work in the home—only one parent in two-parent welfare fam-ilies is obliged to engage in "work activities" under the law.[10] In other words, *the PRA's work provisions permit full-time care-giving where there are two parents, but forbid it where there is only one.*

The work provisions of the Personal Responsibility Act are written in gender-neutral language, so of course the primary care-giving parent in a two-parent welfare family could be the father. However, we know that poor women earn low wages and that families in which mothers are sole providers are disproportionately poor: 60 percent of all poor families with children are single-mother families; and among solo mothers who support their children mainly through their earnings, 60 percent earn a poverty level income ($13,330 for a family of three in 1997) or below.[11] The median family income of single mothers with children under age eighteen was nearly at the poverty line in 1991—half the median family income of solo fathers with minor children and one-fourth that of married couples.[12] During the campaign to end welfare, policymakers frequently pointed to the high rate of maternal and child poverty in single-mother families to explain the need for reform. But rather than target mothers' low wages for improvement, policymakers aimed to recover the absent paternal wage—either through child support or by restoring father-mother families. It is fair to conclude, then, that while the PRA does not require mothers in two-parent families to stay at home, it certainly assumes that where two parents divide the roles of earning and care-giving, it will be the father who brings home the bacon while the mother tends to the children.

The differential based on marital status in the application of work requirements is further evidence that the PRA's primary goal is to restore the system of gender relations in which men pay for families while women raise them. Where welfare policy once compensated families that lacked a male breadwinner, the PRA punishes them. For the unmarried mother enrolled in welfare, compulsory outside work gives a taste of how hard

**107**

Why Should Poor Single Mothers Have to Work Outside the Home?

daily life will be if she is still unmarried when her benefits expire. For the unmarried mother who exhausts her welfare eligibility, full-time wage work is the price of her incorrigible independence. A single mother who wishes to care for her children has little choice but to form a two-parent family with a male wage-earner.

I don't mean to suggest, though, that work requirements are wholly auxiliary to the PRA's aim of restoring the father-mother family. Work requirements are widely popular in themselves as constraints on laziness, disincentives to further childbearing, and preparation for economic self-sufficiency—in short, as correctives for the various depravities catalogued in the rhetoric of welfare dependency. As President Clinton's domestic policy adviser, Bruce Reed, explained: "We believe that kids who grow up in a household without the structure of work as a discipline and aspiration will . . . suffer. . . . If you can bring work to a household and a community, lives will improve."[13] Work requirements provided particularly sturdy ground upon which welfare reformers in both parties could forge consensus. Democrats and Republicans might well disagree about punishing teenage pregnancy or recipient childbearing; but they can and did agree that mothers who continue to need welfare ought to work outside the home.

Work requirements burden mothers least able to bear their weight. Single-mother families have fewer adult resources than do father-mother families—fewer economic resources and fewer human resources to fulfill the responsibility that distinguishes *parents* from other adults, namely care-giving. Moving a poor single mother into the labor market deprives her family of a care-giver; it also deprives the mother of her right to assess family exigencies and to manage her children's home life—in short, to parent. The law obliges single mothers with children under age six to leave them for twenty hours per week regardless of circumstance, and mothers with children over age six to do so nearly full-time (thirty hours per week by 2000).[14] The end of welfare—time limits—is compulsory *full-time* wage-earning, even for mothers of very young children, for poor women cannot support families in low-wage, part-time jobs.

This negation of care-giving by single mothers is the cardinal achievement of the new welfare law. The law does not prescribe outside work as a serious alternative to welfare, for it does not "make work pay" with wage protections and social supports. Rather, the law prescribes outside work to make single mothers pay—pay for daring to be mothers though they be single and poor. The punitive and coercive provisions of the law raise serious questions. What are the practical effects of coerced outside work for poor single mothers and their families? How do those effects promote or forestall equality? If work is an "activity in which one exerts strength or faculties to do or perform something"[15]—if working means being of use—don't single mothers already "work," whether as care-givers or as market laborers and whether they earn welfare or wages?

## The Problem of Outside Work

The premise of the new welfare law is that if the care-giver is unmarried, *any* outside job is better than caring for her own children. The best evidence of this premise is contained in the PRA's list of twelve "work activities" in which at least one parent must engage under the mandatory work rule (see note 2). Culminating the list is "the provision of child care services to an individual who is participating in a community service program."[16] This seriously compromises the work exemption for mothers who cannot find child care. (How can you not find child care when your sister recipients get credit for providing

**109**

Why Should Poor Single Mothers Have to Work Outside the Home?

it? And how can you not find child care when cash-strapped states are encouraging recipients to tend to other recipients' children?[17]) It also insults a single mother's relationship with her own children by giving social approval to her care-giving work only when it is provided for other people's children.

Either explicitly or by omission, other aspects of the mandatory work rule confirm the any-job-will-do approach to welfare reform. For example, unremunerated participation in a community service program counts as a work activity.[18] This is work for work's sake, hardly honing a recipient's income skills and potential. Community service work is usually menial work: raking leaves in public parks, picking up litter on city streets, washing dishes in school cafeterias—tasks recipients already know how to do.[19] Recipients with few educational credentials and weak English language skills (or those who speak with accents) are especially prone to menial assignments, which isolate them from future income opportunities. Further, because such work is performed for free as a condition of welfare eligibility, it is unrewarded by the Earned Income Tax Credit, a federal measure geared to enhance the income of the wage-earning poor.[20]

Beyond its effects on poor mothers, the community service provision undermines the labor market by enticing budget-conscious state and local governments to shift to unpaid labor for menial work. Although the law prohibits the direct substitution of welfare recipients for currently paid workers,[21] some localities have evaded the letter of the law simply by not renewing expired employment contracts with paid workers. Workfare programs, under which recipients are required to work off their benefits, can thus displace paid workers; furthermore, they can choke off income opportunities for welfare recipients who might have been hired into new vacancies as paid workers.[22] On-the-job-training, another permissible work activity, threatens similar effects. The law does not stipulate that trainees be remunerated for work that was once performed by wage-earning employees. In many localities, low-wage workers have been displaced by workfare "trainees" working off their welfare benefits at less than the minimum wage—sometimes as little as $1.50 an hour.[23]

For workfare participants as well as for job trainees, the PRA does not even require welfare agencies and employers to calculate the value of a recipient's work based on the minimum wage. However, the Clinton administration issued a ruling in May 1997 that welfare recipients who are "employees" as defined by the Fair Labor Standards Act are covered by minimum wage laws.[24] This was an important decision for recipients who must work off their benefits, for according to the decision states must value recipients' work at the equivalent of at least the minimum wage. In practical terms, this means that states must calculate the number of hours workfare participants can be compelled to work each month by dividing the family's monthly grant by $5.15. Workfare participants who receive $500 each month in welfare benefits would have to work outside the home 97 hours each month, or about 20 hours each week. If states require recipients to work longer hours (as they will have to under the PRA) they will have to increase benefits.

Unfortunately, the Administration's decision was not based on any specific provision of welfare law. Rather, the Administration interpreted the PRA's repeal of the old welfare system to mean that the old law's provision exempting participants in Community Work Experience Programs from minimum wage standards had also been repealed. At this writing, it is not clear whether the Administration's interpretation will survive attack from Republican governors and members of Congress. In June 1997, Republicans announced plans to quash the minimum

111

Why Should Poor Single Mothers Have to Work Outside the Home?

wage rule by specifically excluding workfare participants from minimum wage and other guarantees of the Fair Labor Standards Act "or any other Federal law."[25] During the 1997 budget reconciliation process, congressional Republicans tried to amend the PRA toward this end, but the White House successfully beat back their effort. Shortly after the budget bill became law, however, Republican leaders vowed to accomplish their objective in separate legislation in the fall of 1997.[26]

The seduction of cheap or "free" labor, combined with the requirement that states enroll increasing numbers of welfare recipients in work, has produced gross exploitation and immiserated low-wage workers who have lost their jobs: in Baltimore, for example, nine public schools hired welfare recipients at $1.50 an hour, terminating contracts with workers who had earned $6 an hour.[27] By mid-1997, some one thousand workers in Baltimore had lost jobs to workfare trainees, dealing a severe blow to workers who had only two years before won a city ordinance guaranteeing a living wage to anyone employed under contracts with the city.[28] Likewise in New York City, thousands of workfare participants now do the work once done by higher-paid city workers.[29]

It is hard to see how the PRA's work requirements promote economic self-sufficiency, the putative alternative to welfare dependency. In addition to neglecting basic earnings guarantees for recipients, the law does not invest in services that improve income opportunities. It limits vocational education to one year; limits the number of adult recipients who may be enrolled in vocational education; withdraws the Family Support Act's encouragement of higher education; does not provide basic education for adults—English as a second language, for example—unless that education is specifically related to employment; and does not adequately fund job training. As a result, the law sentences poor women to low-wage jobs, jobs that paid recipients an average wage of $4.40 per hour in 1990 dollars.[30] Even under the newly increased minimum wage ($5.15 per hour), low-wage workers working forty hours a week all year will not be able to raise their families above poverty.[31]

Moreover, the work provisions do not create jobs—a serious omission since there are not enough existing jobs to absorb four million adults currently receiving welfare. In California, for example, even before the Personal Responsibility Act kicked in, there were one million people, most of whom were not on welfare, looking for jobs; another million who were not counted in the labor force but wanted to be; and nearly a half-million part-time workers who wanted to work more hours. State employment forecasts predict that about 300,000 new jobs will be created annually, *if* the state's economy continues to improve. Even under this optimistic scenario, however, there will not be enough jobs for those who want them, or for those who must have them under the new welfare law.[32]

Jobs that do exist often don't provide self-supporting wages, particularly for poor women, in part because poor women are routinely tracked into low-wage jobs—clerical work, retail sales, food service, cleaning. These jobs are among the most likely to pay subminimum wages: in 1990 dollars, food service jobs paid an average of $3.73 per hour, sales paid $3.94, and cleaning paid $4.08.[33] In addition, many of these jobs, especially service jobs, are not full-time.[34] Even when they pay more than the minimum wage, part-time jobs available to poor women usually will not support their families. A part-time worker who earns $7 an hour and works thirty hours a week, year-round, will not earn more than $10,920 per year. As a recent detailed study of mothers in poverty revealed, wage-earning single mothers with skills and education comparable to mothers receiving welfare are often worse off *because they are*

**113**

Why Should Poor Single Mothers Have to Work Outside the Home?

*earning wages.* While gross family incomes are higher for wage earners, income gains from wage-earning are eaten up by the costs of clothing for work, transportation, and child care. The expenses of wage-earning leave little to pay for any but the most immediate necessities—food and rent. Hence, 40 percent of wage-earning single mothers lack health insurance.[35]

The location of jobs further undermines the work solution to welfare. Jobs are increasingly inaccessible to the communities that need them. New York City, for example, which had 300,000 adults on welfare in 1995, has lost 227,000 jobs since 1990.[36] In Chicago, nine out of ten jobs available in manufacturing are far from where recipients reside, sometimes outside city limits. This is also true of the service jobs available through United Airlines and United Parcel Service, two companies President Clinton challenged by name to employ welfare recipients in his 1997 State of the Union Message. Recipients employed in these jobs must often travel an hour or more, transferring among buses or trains, just to get to work.[37]

The Personal Responsibility Act does not make work pay, or even make work available. Yet it insists that single mothers are worth more outside their homes than in them, and so erects significant barriers to care-giving by single mothers for their own children. The foremost barrier, of course, is time: work outside the home restricts time for nurturing, counseling, talking, checking homework, cleaning, shopping, cooking, sewing, meeting teachers, attending school plays, not to mention caring for children when they are ill. Single mothers' loss of home time directly injures children's welfare: work outside the home creates stretches of time during which children may not receive any care and supervision at all, for poor mothers with little education and job training often have nonstandard work schedules, which do not coincide with schedules for formal child care.[38] The PRA does not acknowledge children's need for care, let alone single mothers' right to assure it. Instead, the Act repeals the child care entitlement for recipients, terminates welfare-related child care programs, and falls $1 billion short of providing enough child care funding to meet the needs of mothers it compels to work outside the home.[39]

The PRA's stinginess on child care follows from its supporters' preference for married mothers. As the exemption of married mothers from mandatory work shows, welfare law assumes that where there are two parents there is no need for child care. According to this logic, parents who need child care will mostly be single mothers, whom the law intends to burden rather than assist. Although the welfare law purports to be the Personal Responsibility and *Work Opportunity* Act, it fosters no work opportunities and makes work outside the home unaffordable for poor single mothers. Poor families already spend 27 percent of their monthly income on child care (as compared to 7 percent spent by families with incomes above the poverty line).[40] After child care expenses, a single mother working full-time at minimum wage will bring home a net annual income of $7,972!

The law is likewise stingy in accommodating the needs of domestic violence victims. The Family Violence Amendment authored by Senators Paul Wellstone (D-Minnesota) and Patti Murray (D-Washington) clearly improved the PRA by permitting states to waive certain requirements for domestic violence victims. But it doesn't oblige states to do so.[41] Moreover, while states are permitted to waive time limits, they are not specifically permitted to waive work requirements. This is a serious problem: studies report that among mothers in welfare-to-work programs, 56 percent are abused by male partners, and that recipients' return to the labor market often triggers new violence.[42] Recipients' entry into the labor market also

**115**

Why Should Poor Single Mothers Have to Work Outside the Home?

vitiates their escape to battered women's shelters: work requirements remove women from shelters to which abusers are denied access and put them in unprotected work sites where abusers can stalk, harass, or hurt them. Mothers who will need the domestic violence exception generally will be mothers who have left or are leaving relationships with men, often the fathers of their children. By extending them parsimonious protections and then only at the pleasure of state governments, the law further disdains mothers who decide to parent alone.

Harsh and uncompromising work rules for unmarried mothers, along with time limits, result from welfare reformers' syllogistic correlation of such mothers' marital status with their need for welfare. This singular view erases the diversity of poor women's circumstances—the diversity of their families' needs, and the diversity of their potential to earn a living wage. It also ignores a wealth of data documenting the fact that it is not for lack of desire to participate in the labor market that single mothers turn to welfare, but because responsible parenting impels them to do so.

From researchers who have listened to recipients we learn that many different life events and needs can precipitate and sustain the need for welfare: divorce, abuse, disability, a sick child, unaffordable child care, lack of health insurance, poverty wages, rigid jobs. We learn that single mothers meet the challenges of poverty variously, depending on the availability of kin, education, transportation, and support services like child care. And we learn that for most single mothers who need welfare, care-giving is their first priority, one that often conflicts with work outside the home. One author explained: "They view the world through the lens of motherhood. . . . They do not see themselves as providers, struggling to be a parent within that context. Rather, they view themselves as mothers, and struggle to be providers within *that* context."[43]

Many recipients already take that struggle into the labor market. In fact, although welfare politicians maintained that recipients don't and won't work—that they need to be forcibly "moved" into jobs—evidence indicates that even before the PRA forced them to, 43 percent of recipients either combined wages with welfare or cycled between the two.[44] Data also show, however, that single mothers have often been unable to trade welfare for wages permanently, though not for lack of will and effort. The reason is that they are strapped for cash *and* strapped for time. Without living wages, guaranteed child care, or health benefits at work, and without time-saving amenities at home—a car, a washing machine, a vacuum cleaner, or even a phone—basic maintenance of children and households presents Herculean challenges.

Some mothers have met these challenges while working outside the home and will continue to. But for others, responsibility for children simply cannot be reconciled with wage-earning. What is a mother with a disabled or sick child to do, for example? Hope that a young sibling will make the right emergency medical decisions? Gamble that a potentially fatal asthma attack won't come? Assume that a mentally retarded child can amuse herself safely and beneficially for eight or ten hours at a stretch? Or entrust her to a teenage baby-sitter, who welfare law says is too irresponsible to parent her own children?

One mother described her dilemma: "All the years she was growing up, I couldn't work. You never know when she would get sick. If she had a seizure in school someone had to pick her up. I couldn't give that responsibility to someone else. . . . It might be today. It might be tomorrow. She might get sick for two days straight or she might not get sick for another week.

117

Why Should Poor Single Mothers Have to Work Outside the Home?

Would a boss understand that?"[45] Another mother explained that though she tried to work outside the home she soon discovered that her child's needs conflicted with her employer's schedule: "I was working at the dog-bone factory. My daughter had so many problems with her ears. She has had tubes in and out. . . . She had gotten sick when I was working and I missed work and I kept missing work because of taking her to the doctors and getting her operations done, and I got fired."[46] Such complexities at home and consequent vulnerabilities in the labor market will not disappear just because welfare law ignores them.

The difficulties faced by poor single mothers with disabled or chronically ill children may not be typical, but they are instructive. Hardship creates stark and often unresolvable conflicts between outside work and care-giving. For single mothers who are poor—as for single or married mothers who are better off—wage-earning remains a privilege, affordable for those who can hire surrogate care-givers and costly for those who cannot.

## Why Should Poor Single Mothers Have to Work Outside the Home?

Charles Murray inflamed the campaign to end welfare in 1984 when he purported to show how the economic incentive to receive welfare destroyed the moral values of an imaginary couple named Harold and Phyllis.[47] The claim that welfare encouraged illegitimacy and sloth became the rallying cry for welfare foes. Murray and others argued that welfare was not only more profitable than marriage, but more profitable than wages as well. A recent study by the Cato Institute captured this reasoning. The authors maintained (against detailed refutation by the Center for Budget and Policy Priorities) that "the full package of benefits"—AFDC, food stamps, Medicaid, housing assistance, utilities assistance, the Women, Infants, and Children (WIC) program, and the free commodities program— "actually provides recipients with incomes above the poverty level in every state. The value, relative to a job providing the same after-tax income, ranges from $36,400 in Hawaii to $11,500 in Mississippi. In eight jurisdictions . . . welfare pays at least the equivalent of a $25,000-a-year job."[48] Throughout the welfare debate, welfare foes cited this sort of data as evidence of welfare's perverse incentives. Opposing work to welfare, "a job" to a free ride, they called for strong controls on the conditions and duration of benefits.

The controls enacted in the Personal Responsibility Act create a unique statutory obligation for poor single mothers to work outside the home. This formalizes inequality among women: we do not oblige, nor even expect, married mothers to work outside the home. To be sure, many do work outside the home—some out of economic necessity, others for personal fulfillment, still others to avoid economic dependence on husbands. But none work outside the home because the law tells them to. Moreover, data show that most married mothers, left with a choice not to work outside the home, make that choice at least part of the time.

Most married mothers with children under age eighteen are not full-time, full-year wage-earners. Among all married mothers, only 36.8 percent worked full-time, full-year in 1992, while 11.2 percent worked all year, but part-time.[49] Where fathers were fully employed, only 29.5 percent of mothers were full-time, full-year wage-earners. Less than a third (30.6 percent) of all married mothers with children under age six worked full-time and all year in 1992. Less than *one-quarter* (24.3 percent) of married mothers with children under age six whose husbands were full-time wage-earners earned full-time, full-year wages themselves. White married mothers had lower overall rates of full-time, full-year work (35.6 percent) than did Black married mothers (49.1 percent).[50]

Clearly, most married mothers do not produce family-supporting wages—because most married mothers are only partially and intermittently employed outside the home. This is especially true where fathers are fully employed, even though higher incomes in such families and the presence of two adults can attenuate some of the worst trade-offs between wage-earning and care-giving. Much has been made of increases in women's labor force participation since AFDC was created in 1935 to justify repealing welfare's support for mothers' care-giving work in the home. Certainly changes have been dramatic, especially for married mothers: in 1992, 72.9 percent worked outside the home at some point during the year, as compared to 51.3 percent in 1970.[51] But alongside these changes run two fundamental continuities: most married mothers do not sacrifice care-giving to wage-earning, as their labor force patterns seem to accommodate family needs; and one-third of married mothers with children under six do not participate in the labor force at all.[52]

Some married mothers, including some with young children, undoubtedly would like to work more hours and earn more wages. But discrimination in the labor market and the lack of family-friendly labor policies such as child care and paid parental leave constrain their choices. Other married mothers feel that they "have to" work outside the home more than they want to—to supplement a father's low wages, for example, or to maintain the family's standard of living while saving for a child's education or paying off a mortgage. But although their choices about outside work may be constrained by the labor market or by economic necessity, society does not expect married mothers to work outside the home. Nor does social policy say that they must. If there is an expectation imposed on married mothers, it is rather that they should choose care-giving over wage-earning, if they can afford at all to make that choice. While this expectation reflects conventional thinking about gender roles, it also expresses social approval for, and assigns social value to, married mothers' care-giving work in the home.

Such approval does not exist for the care-giving work of poor single mothers, in part because they *are* poor and single, and in part because the poor single mother of popular imagination is Black. Some people point to the material and moral circumstances of poor single mothers to question the quality of their care-giving work and, thus, to dispute its value. Some conclude that poor single mothers ought not to raise their own children. Especially where Black single mothers are at issue, some argue that poor unmarried women ought not to bear children at all. Hence welfare law's provisions to prevent non-marital births: incentive payments to states to reduce "illegitimacy," and abstinence education targeted against "groups which are most likely to bear children out-of-wedlock." And hence work requirements that force mothers into the labor market, where they have a harder time caring for children and where they are supposed to have fewer births.

Racial politics propelled welfare reform, suggesting measures that are particularly harmful to women of color and thus further racialize inequality among women. Although welfare policy aims indiscriminately at poor mothers who are not married, it does so with decidedly racial effects. African American and Latina mothers are disproportionately poor, and, accordingly, disproportionately enrolled in welfare: in 1994, adult recipients in AFDC families were 37.4 percent white, 36.4 percent Black, 19.9 percent Latina, 2.9 percent Asian, and 1.3 percent Native American. Moreover, of non-marital mothers who receive welfare, only 28.4 percent are white.[53] Hence, the burdens that welfare law imposes on mothers because they are not married are burdens that fall especially heavily on women of color.

At the crossroads of race, morality, and poverty, welfare law codifies disdain for poor single mothers *as mothers*. Two recent events exemplify and harden this disdain. The first was the 1997 White House Conference on Early Child Development, which showcased extensive findings documenting the stunning impact of spoken language on infant and child brain development.[54] The conferees urged parents to spend more and better time with their children—to be more talkative (2,000 words an hour will make your child smarter) and to seek stimulating and articulate child care providers if they must work outside the home. Citing the findings, some Clinton advisers have called for tax incentives to make it easier for parents to stay at home.[55] But no one called for policies that would make it easier for poor single mothers to stay at home; and no one voiced concern that lawmakers' prescriptions for poor single mothers contradict experts' prescriptions for children. In fact, one Clinton official insisted that when it comes to welfare families, wage work is more important than care-giving, the moral discipline of mothers more important than the intellectual growth of children.[56]

Some experts buttressed this view with studies showing that welfare mothers are least likely to positively affect their children's development. Apparently, in comparison to professional and working-class parents, welfare mothers were least likely to speak volubly to their children (only 600 words an hour).[57] Although this finding should support claims for guaranteed, verbally stimulating (and probably expensive) child care services for welfare mothers' children, no one has used the White House conference as a springboard for making such a claim. Instead, states continue to encourage reputedly monosyllabic welfare recipients to become child care providers for other recipients' children—as a cheap alternative to publicly provided care.

In Congress, meanwhile, legislation to facilitate adoption provided a second occasion to repudiate poor single motherhood. Introduced by House Republicans, the proposal may make it even more difficult for some poor single mothers to retain custody of their children. Welfare law already endangers poor single mothers' constitutional right to parent their own children because it creates circumstances that tempt authorities to remove children to foster care. Moreover, while the PRA removes the welfare entitlement, it retains child protection provisions that entitle children to foster care. Under these provisions, parents who lose welfare and cannot earn wages sufficient to support children could lose their children because states are obliged to protect children from maltreatment, including the effects of poverty.[58]

Mere compliance with the welfare law's work provisions makes single mothers vulnerable to child removal policies. Time required in the labor market, either by rule or by necessity, diminishes the time available for care. Low wages do not pay for child care, leaving children potentially untended if they are not in school. Low wages do not pay for after care, leaving children in many instances to fend for themselves in unsafe neighborhoods or in dwellings with poor security. Nor do low wages pay for food, rent, and health insurance for children, let alone for clothing and transportation for their mother to get to work. For these and other reasons, even a mother who obeys all the rules risks subjecting her child to some degree of deprivation. Some mothers are so poor they cannot afford heat, electricity, or even shelter. Time limits will make mothers' and children's need more acute, and increase the risk of utter destitution. Some poor mothers will have to place their children

**123**

Why Should Poor Single Mothers Have to Work Outside the Home?

temporarily in foster care until they recover from an illness or until they can find a way to pay for necessities. When case-workers interpret maternal poverty as maternal neglect, others will lose their children to child welfare agencies.

Until 1997, mothers who surrendered their children under these circumstances had some chance of getting them back; child welfare law favored family reunification and thus presumed that poor mothers would eventually resume custody.[59] Now, however, Congress has made it easier to remove children from their mothers' homes *permanently*. In 1997, the Congress enacted the Adoption and Safe Families Act, facilitating adoption in two crucial ways that are pertinent to our consideration of welfare.[60] First, the act speeds the termination of parental rights where children are under age ten and have been in foster care for fifteen out of twenty-two months (a time limit on parental rights that is *shorter* than the time limit on welfare). Second, the act urges states to increase adoption rates for foster children by offering them a $4,000 bounty for each adoption that exceeds the number of placements accomplished the previous year.[61] This bounty gives states incentive not only to terminate parental rights swiftly, but to put ever increasing numbers of foster children up for adoption, as well. One of the measure's few opponents described its connections to welfare law this way: "First you take their money away. Then you force them into desperate conditions of poverty. Then you deem them unfit to raise their children . . . and place [the children] in foster homes. Then after 18 months you put the children up for adoption. Whose family values do we stand for?"[62]

Welfare law and the adoption law bespeak profound contempt for care-giving if it is performed by mothers who are poor and unmarried. That contempt becomes even more evident if we examine other policies affecting care-giving by mothers: social policy draws distinctions not only *against* disdained mothers, but also *in favor* of mothers who enjoy social approval.

In contrast with welfare law, survivors' insurance (SI) gives widowed mothers "a choice between staying at home to care for the child and working."[63] A provision added to the Social Security Act in 1939, SI provides monthly cash benefits to the widows and children of covered workers. Though the language of SI is now gender neutral, like welfare it was invented for mothers; not until 1975 did widowed fathers become eligible for benefits.[64] Moreover, its effects remain gendered even today: 278,000 widowed mothers received benefits in 1992 as compared to 16,000 widowed fathers.[65]

The burdens of care-giving and providing fall on unmarried mothers as well as on widows, but social policy addresses those burdens differently because widows were once married. Where the welfare law tells unmarried mothers to get to work outside the home, SI underwrites the widowed mother's decision to devote herself to the care of her children. Moreover, SI rewards a mother for *ever* having been married to her children's deceased father: even if she is divorced she may receive benefits, as long as she is not currently remarried.

Survivors' insurance enjoys legitimacy because it provides for widows and half-orphans—blameless victims of family tragedy. It is also supported by the fiction that an insured, deceased worker's survivors are "getting back" what he paid in Social Security taxes. But benefits do not correlate with contributions: for instance, a worker who retires at age sixty-five consumes his Social Security contributions within three years. The family of a worker who dies at age forty likely consumes his contributions faster still: not only has the deceased worker paid in for fewer years, but each surviving child and the mother receive individual benefits equal to three-fourths of the deceased's primary insurance amount (up to a monthly family maximum).[66] A mother may collect benefits until no child is under age sixteen, and each child may collect benefits until age eighteen (or nineteen if enrolled in elementary or secondary school). In other words, at some point survivors' benefits become "welfare," or a socially provided income.

But survivors' benefits are not stigmatized, do not carry conditions that invite governmental intrusion into mothers' lives, and do not stipulate that mothers must work outside the home. The only time limits that apply are the dependent child's impending adulthood. Furthermore, benefits are pegged to a national scale and are far more generous than welfare. The average monthly benefit for a child was $460 in 1995, and the average mother's benefit was $485.[67] A surviving child of a worker who earned the minimum wage in each year used in the computation of the benefit and who died in 1995 at age forty was eligible for $405 each month; a mother and one child together were eligible for $810. The surviving widow and two children of a father who earned the national average wage each year ($24,673 in 1995) received $1,617 in monthly benefits—just shy of their maximum family benefit of $1,619. The survivors of a father who earned maximum Social Security wages each year ($61,200 in 1995) were entitled to a maximum monthly family benefit of $2,473.[68]

Though more generous than welfare, survivors' benefits do not wholly compensate for the loss of the deceased's wages—especially for survivors of a worker who earned more than $61,200 per year. Nor do benefits raise the survivors of low-wage workers out of poverty. However, the SI system permits beneficiaries to augment the family stipend with wages of up to $8,280 per year without affecting benefits. Thus widowed mothers may, as most married mothers do, work outside the home part-time to enhance the family income. The widow of a minimum-wage worker can raise her family's income to $18,000 in this way; the widow of a worker who earned the national average wage can raise her family's income to $27,684. After the first $8,280 in outside earnings, family benefits are reduced by $1 for every $2 earned.

Contrast all this with welfare policy. Survivors' insurance enables mothers to choose to work inside the home, and its liberal earnings exemption permits mothers to strike a balance between wage-earning and care-giving if they want to. Welfare law, on the other hand, not only commands recipients to work outside the home, it provides benefits too low to survive on while making it impossible to earn one's way out of poverty by combining benefits with wages. Even before the Personal Responsibility Act, the most generous states (except Alaska and Hawaii) never provided recipients more than $690 in monthly benefits for a family of three. And both federal and state policy treated outside income as the direct replacement for welfare. SI beneficiaries can earn $690 each month without penalty to benefits, and can retain partial (if declining) benefits on income above that amount. But welfare recipients in twenty-four states lost their eligibility for *any* benefits if their outside monthly income ranged from $366 (Alabama) to $756 (Georgia) in 1995; recipients in another fifteen states lost eligibility when their monthly income exceeded the $750–950 range.[69] In most states, recipients are kicked off welfare even when their earnings are well below the poverty threshold.[70]

Survivors' insurance tells certain mothers that taxpayers will support them should they choose to work inside the home or boost their wages should they choose not to. Indeed, "'mothers' insurance benefits' were intended to make the choice to stay at home easier."[71] Accordingly, SI invests in care-giving directly, guaranteeing benefits for mothers until their youngest child has reached age sixteen; and it supports care-giving indi-rectly, guaranteeing benefits to children until age eighteen (or nineteen, if still in high school). Welfare law sends precisely the opposite message to poor single mothers: they might receive income support, if their state deems it appropriate, but at most for five years and then only if they move into the labor market nearly full-time; moreover, they will receive no support for the work that they do raising their children. The survivors' insur-ance system has its flaws: it repeats income inequalities by pegging survivors' benefits to the deceased's wages, for exam-ple. Further, although survivors' insurance supports some mothers' work in the home, it does not directly pay for it: benefits are a surrogate for fathers' wages, not compensation for mothers' work. Nevertheless, survivors' insurance estab-lishes three important principles. First, it formally recognizes that a lone parent has decisions to make about care-giving and wage-earning. Second, it demonstrates that one purpose of so-cial policy is to underwrite the "opportunity for choice"[72]— that is, to make it feasible for lone parents, usually mothers, to choose *not* to earn wages. Third, it designates care-giving as a socially necessary and valuable activity, deserving of social assistance.

Since we already value the care-giving work performed by some mothers, it should not require a huge conceptual leap to value the care-giving work performed by poor single moth-ers. What it does take is a leap across the divide of racial-ized morality to separate the work of care-giving from the marital circumstances under which it is performed. If we do not take the leap across this divide, we ask poor single mothers to earn equality by surrendering their rights—by refusing motherhood if they are poor and single. If we do not take the leap across this divide, we sentence poor single mothers to eugenic social policy, rather than accord them full and equal citizenship.

## Work and Welfare

The repudiation of poor single mothers' care-giving work has stirred few objections, even among opponents of the Personal Responsibility Act. Although President Clinton initially opposed the PRA, for example, he promised to be "tough on work" and heartily endorsed work requirements: his own welfare bill contained precisely such requirements, as well as time limits to back them up.[73] Among liberal critics of work requirements, arguments generally have stressed that workfare does not prepare recipients for decent jobs, that job opportunities do not exist, that outside work is impractical in the absence of affordable child care, and that work requirements for welfare recipients threaten the jobs of other low-wage workers.[74] These arguments contest the PRA's methods of moving recipients from welfare to work, but they do not refute the idea that poor single mothers *should* seek work outside the home. Many feminists, meanwhile, bristle at the coercion in work requirements, but nevertheless favor wage work as the solution to welfare. They call for family-friendly labor market reforms—universal child care, paid parental leave, pay equity—to pave the way from welfare to work.[75] Except for welfare rights activists and a handful of feminists, no one has defended poor mothers' right to raise their children, and no one has questioned the assumption that poor single mothers should *have to* work outside the home.[76]

At least not lately. In 1973, a special task force convened by President Nixon's secretary of Health, Education, and Welfare issued a report assessing various social problems in terms of work. Among its conclusions was the call "to give full recognition to the fact that keeping house and raising children is work, and it is as difficult to do well . . . as paid jobs producing goods and services."[77] Finding that family care-givers, usually women, routinely spend an average of forty hours a week on housework, the task force reasoned: "Thus, subsidies to AFDC mothers could well be justified as payments for non-market work rather than as a dole in lieu of 'work'."[78] The task force continued: "The choice confronting the AFDC mother [sh]ould no longer be between taking a job or receiving no assistance (which is really no choice at all) but rather the choice between working at home, in her own house with her own children, or working outside the home. In the long run, such a change in the choice offered to welfare mothers would not only cost less, but it would also permit the welfare family to keep its self-respect and at the same time enlarge an important area of choice in our society."[79]

Far from recognizing welfare mothers as workers, however, welfare reformers have insisted that the work such mothers do raising children is of no use to the rest of us. Even as the Task Force on Work in America called for social recognition for unpaid care-giving work, Richard Nixon, Ronald Reagan, Southern Democrats, and others drummed up hostility toward care-givers who need welfare because they are poor and parenting alone. Across thirty years, anti-welfare politicians and the public whose resentments they captured transposed mothers who need welfare into "cheats" and "queens" and "breeders"; not surprisingly, the program that originated to support care-givers was transformed, in the public imagination, into a program that paid lazy, immoral mothers to do nothing. Ending welfare "as a way of life" thus came to mean ending care-giving as a way of work for mothers who are poor and single. More-over, it came to mean institutionalizing such mothers as a caste of providers for other people—of goods, services, and *care* for other people and their children.

There may be some cracks in the discourse, however. Re-publicans recently attached a work requirement to public hous-ing assistance, mandating adult tenants to perform volunteer work as a condition of residence,[80] but most Democrats voted for an amendment sponsored by Representative Jesse Jackson, Jr. (D-Illinois) to exempt from this requirement single parents with children under age six. Many Democrats argued not only that compulsory volunteer work constituted involuntary servi-tude and anyway contradicted the meaning of "volunteer," but that it disrespected the work performed by care-givers, as well. As one Democrat, who had supported workfare for welfare recipients the year before, intoned: "The truth of the matter is I think we should be encouraging mothers and families to take care of their children in their own homes and valuing that as a society. . . . I thought that was, as a matter of fact, one of the core values we were trying to encourage in this country—not to go take children off to somebody else's home but to bring them up ourselves. And why is that not an effort? Why is that not a reasonable effort and one that should qualify under the gentleman's notion of [work]?"[81]

It is time to apply equality standards to our discourse, as well as to our laws—to test our descriptions of and prescriptions for others against their consequences for rights, choices, and dig-nity. Why do we view welfare mothers as "loafers"? Because our expectations of women of color—of Black women bowed over in the fields, of Asian women hunched over sewing ma-chines, of Latinas kneeling down on our kitchen floors—is that they are workers, not mothers? Why do we mark marriage as the boundary between deserving and undeserving mothers, at

**131**

Why Should Poor Single Mothers Have to Work Outside the Home?

least for mothers who are poor? Because we fear mothers' independence, in personal relations and as citizens? Why do we vaunt care-giving only for mothers with means or men? Because it permits us to sustain a distinction between "the dole" and social security—to separate poor single mothers as a subject caste from rights-bearing citizens of the welfare state? If we interrogate what we say, we will recant what we have legislated, for I trust that most Americans do not believe that race, or gender, or class castes are compatible with democratic citizenship.

# 5

## After Welfare's End

The Personal Responsibility and Work Opportunity Act of 1996 locked poor single mothers in a police state that steals their rights and denies them income security. The welfare police state provides cash assistance, food stamps, and Medicaid to poor single mothers and their children, but only if mothers reveal their most intimate relations to government, only if they agree to associate with the men whom government designates as their children's fathers, and only if they forfeit the right to care for their own children. In exchange for welfare, recipients must surrender vocational freedom, sexual privacy, and reproductive choice, as well as the right to make decisions about how to be and to raise a family. Ordinarily, these rights are strongly guarded by constitutional doctrine, as they form the core of the Supreme Court's jurisprudence of (heterosexual) personhood and family. Not so for a mother who needs welfare.

The most talked-about aspect of the new welfare regime is its "dramaturgy of work,"[1] but the regime's foremost objective is to restore the patriarchal family. The Temporary Assistance for Needy Families program (TANF), the welfare system established by the PRA in 1996, includes numerous provisions that promote marriage and paternal headship while frustrating childbearing and child-raising rights outside of marriage. TANF's impositions on the right of poor mothers to form and sustain their own families—as well as to avoid or exit from untenable relationships with men—proceed from the stiff paternity establishment and child support rules discussed in chapter 3. The *2000 Green Book*, published by the House Committee on Ways and Means, boasts that TANF's "exceptionally strong paternity establishment requirements" constitute its most direct attack on independent motherhood; the requirement that mothers cooperate in establishing and enforcing child support orders as a condition of receiving welfare, meanwhile, impairs mothers' ability to remain independent.[2] If mothers do not obey these rules, they lose part or all of their families' benefits.

The TANF welfare regime enforces these interventions into poor single mothers' intimate relationships by compelling mothers to work outside the home if they remain single. Mothers who are married do not have to work outside the home, even though they receive welfare, because labor market work by only one parent in a two-parent family satisfies TANF's work requirement.[3] Notwithstanding a decade of rhetoric about moving from welfare to work, the TANF regime treats wage work as the alternative to marriage, not to welfare—as punishment for mothers' independence.

The TANF regime enforces its rules with sanctions, or penalties. Sanction policies have had a striking impact on welfare participation. During the first years of TANF, between 1997 and 1999, 540,000 families lost a TANF check as a result of sanctions. With sanctioned families among the poorest of all former TANF participants, the threat of sanctions warns all recipients to accept the TANF regime's patriarchal rules and labor market punishments as the terms of economic survival.[4]

Under TANF, states must impose financial penalties when an adult recipient does not meet work requirements, does not cooperate in establishing paternity, or does not cooperate in enforcing child support orders. TANF also authorizes, but does not require, penalties when an adult recipient does not comply with the provisions of her "personal responsibility contract," such as when she fails to have her child immunized or to assure her child's satisfactory school attendance.[5] States may make "good cause" exceptions to both federal and state rules, but in practice good cause exceptions are not well known to recipients and are not generously granted by states.

Sanction policies vary among states and among families within states.[6] In thirty-six states, some families suffer a partial reduction of their TANF grant the first time a mother fails to comply with a rule. In twenty of these states, further non-compliance eventually results in the whole family being kicked out of TANF. In eighteen states, some families lose their entire TANF grant the first time an adult recipient fails to comply with a TANF rule. Thirteen states terminate the adult recipient's Medicaid coverage if she is "sanctioned off" TANF for not meeting the work requirement. In most states, when whole families are sanctioned off TANF they frequently also lose their Medicaid coverage—even if they remain eligible for it. Often, such families are not informed of their eligibility; and often, welfare agencies don't do the paperwork necessary to assure that families that have left the TANF system retain health protection. Accordingly, TANF penalties not only breed material vulnerability but endanger families' health, as well.[7]

TANF penalties also endanger mothers' custody of children. Department of Health and Human Services guidelines stipulate that welfare monies may be used to "screen families who have been sanctioned under TANF" to determine whether children are at risk of child abuse or neglect. A mother who does not want child support, or who does not want to identify biological fathers, or who cannot meet the thirty-hour weekly work requirement thus comes under suspicion as an abusive or neglectful parent. If a mother does not "cure" her sanction by coming into compliance, her children may be found to be "at risk" and placed in foster care. If her children are young and remain in foster care for fifteen out of twenty-two months, her parental rights may be terminated.

These injuries of welfare reform are born of poverty but lived through race. About two-thirds of welfare recipients today are African American, Asian American, Latina, and Native American. From the 1960s to the present day, 35 to 40 percent of recipients have been African American; in 1999, 36.4 percent of TANF recipients were Black. Latina and Asian American participation has increased over this period, as the Latino and Asian American populations as a whole have increased. Latina participation in 1999 was 23.1 percent, Asian American participation was 5 percent, and Native American participation was 1.7 percent.[8]

Steeper racial disparities in TANF participation may be in store, as white recipients are leaving the rolls more rapidly than are women of color, and many are not entering the rolls at all. In New York City, for example, the number of whites on welfare declined by 57 percent between 1995 and 1998, while the number of Blacks declined by 30 percent and the number of Latinas by only 7 percent.[9] Nationwide, whites' welfare participation declined by 51 percent during the late 1990s, while African Americans' participation declined by 40 percent and Latinas' by 30 percent.[10] As a result, women of color have increased as a percentage of TANF adults. In twenty-four states, women of color compose more than two-thirds of adult TANF enrollments; in eighteen of those states, they compose three-quarters or more of enrollments.[11]

This racial distribution of TANF participation is the logical consequence of the racial distribution of poverty. Women of color have been and still are poorer than everyone else, single mothers of color even more so. In 1999, 25.4 percent of non-Hispanic white single-mother families lived below the poverty line, while 46.1 percent of African American and 46.6 percent of Latina single-mother families did so.[12] The racial distribution of poverty is enforced by racism and discrimination in most walks of life. In the labor market, for example, African American women who are employed full-time earn only 64 cents to every dollar earned by white men and 84 cents to every white woman's dollar. The wage gap for Latinas is even larger: they earn 55 cents to the white man's dollar and 72 cents to the white woman's.[13]

If the TANF regime's assault on poor mothers' rights wields an unmistakably disparate racial impact, it does so by imposing unmistakable constraints on poor mothers' rights and choices as women. TANF's paternity establishment, child support enforcement, and work requirements primarily target mothers who are not married—because they are not married now and were not married when their children were born.

At least since the 1960s, the attack on non-marital mothers has been loaded with racial stereotypes and driven by racism. Although racially neutral on their face, TANF rules operationalize these dynamics in welfare law. Using marriage and family structure to calibrate its punishments, TANF burdens women of color disproportionately. The total number of non-marital births is highest among white women, but the rate of births per 1,000 unmarried women has been highest among women of color: 73.4 for non-Hispanic Black women and 91.4 for Latinas, as compared to 27 for non-Hispanic white women.[14] The percentage of single-parent families among Blacks (62.3 percent) is more than twice that among whites (26.6 percent), and the percentage of Black families sustained by never-married mothers (36.5 percent) is far greater than the percentage of white families (6.6 percent).[15] Finally, according to the *2000 Green Book*, the poverty rate is highest among "independent families" (57.7 percent) and "cohabiting families" (58 percent) sustained by never-married mothers, among whom women of color figure disproportionately.[16]

The racial distribution of poverty is reflected in the disproportionate presence of non-marital mothers of color on TANF rolls. TANF's patriarchal provisions are therefore racialized in their effects. These effects are not unplanned; by sounding the alarm against "fatherless childrearing," the TANF regime celebrates "the perspicacity of Moynihan's vision" that "[B]lack Americans [are] held back economically and socially in large part because their family structure [is] deteriorating."[17] And so the TANF regime exploits women-of-color poverty to suffocate single mothers' independence.

## Fatherhood and Marriage: The "Next Steps" in Welfare Reform

The disciplinary terms of cash assistance enforce poor single mothers' inequality. One measure of this inequality is the persistence of poverty among mothers who have left TANF. Even among employed former recipients, the median income was only $10,924 in 1999—well below the poverty line of $13,423 for a family of three with two children.[18] Among all former TANF recipients, fifty percent remain in poverty and thirty percent have not found jobs.[19] In many former TANF families, income is so low or so tenuous that families must go hungry, use food pantries, or apply for emergency food assistance.[20] Study after study reports high rates of hardship among former

TANF recipients, hardships that range from having to forgo necessary medical care to being unable to pay the rent or the phone bill.[21] Because poverty is racially distributed, because employers are more likely to hire white recipients, and because welfare agencies tend to treat white recipients more favorably, for instance by informing them of available social supports, post-TANF hardship has a disparate racial impact.[22]

One reason for the persistence of poverty among former TANF recipients is that they have moved primarily into low-wage and contingent jobs without benefits; most are earning only around $7.00 per hour, far below a living wage.[23] Exacerbating the problem of low wages is the lack of social supports for low-income workers. Fewer than one-third of employed former TANF participants have health insurance from their employers, for example. In addition, although many former TANF recipients remain eligible for food stamps and Medicaid, they often lose access to these social supports when they leave TANF. Also, many former recipients end up having to spend 25 to 30 percent of their incomes on child care, for a number of reasons: even though eligible for federal child care assistance, families often are not informed about it; as many as one-quarter of former TANF recipients work night, graveyard, or irregular shifts, when child care is unavailable; and in any case waiting lists are long, as only 10 to 15 percent of eligible children are served by federally subsidized providers.[24]

The national child poverty rate has declined by a percent or two in the five years since TANF replaced AFDC.[25] Although the overall poverty rate has declined in single-mother families in recent years, this improvement does not signal improved economic circumstances among poor children's mothers. Despite the strong economy during the late 1990s, poverty actually has deepened for those who remain poor—that is, mothers who need welfare—and has increased among some wage-earning families.[26] Even among TANF mothers who have "played by the rules"—naming fathers, helping government recover TANF grants by collecting fathers' incomes, and working outside the home for wages—the TANF regime has not provided a pathway out of poverty.

The poverty that haunts single mothers after they leave TANF has provided fodder to right-wing patriarchal Republicans who believe that the TANF regime could do more to promote father-mother family formation. Single-mother poverty also has inspired many Democrats to look to fathers as economic lifelines for mothers. The focus on fathers has led both Republicans and Democrats to propose wage-enhancing services for noncustodial parents of TANF children. It also has led them to urge government to promote marriage.

The 1996 welfare law made father-mother family formation a goal of TANF but did not specify how that was to be accomplished. Paternity establishment and child support provisions pressure mothers to enter into economic relations with biological fathers, but do not guarantee either marriage or residential fatherhood. Nor do these provisions guarantee that fathers will be economically able to meet their statutory obligations. In 1997, Congress addressed some of the gaps in TANF's family policy when it added programs for noncustodial parents to the Welfare-to-Work program.[27] The aim was to enhance biological fathers' ability to support their children.

The Clinton administration further sharpened TANF's patriarchal discipline when it promulgated regulations and initiatives to implement the new welfare law. One Clinton administration program, the Fatherhood Initiative, worked aggressively to improve paternity establishment rates. According to the Department of Health and Human Services, this initiative contributed to the tripling of established paternities between fiscal year 1992 and fiscal year 1998, from 512,000 to 1.5 million.[28] To further promote biological fathers' connections to children, the Clinton administration awarded grants and waivers to states in support of governmental, faith-based, and nonprofit initiatives such as Parents' Fair Share and Partners for Fragile Families, which aim to engage fathers in the legal, emotional, and financial aspects of parenthood.[29]

Complementing its efforts to promote fatherhood, the Clinton administration also encouraged states to use TANF funds to promote marriage. Department of Health and Human Services guidelines point out that TANF's block grants are "extraordinarily flexible" and allow states to *change eligibility rules to provide incentives for single parents to marry or for two-parent families to stay together.*"[30] Eligibility rules for parents who need TANF—mostly single mothers—can include mandatory enrollment in marriage classes and couples counseling; incentives can include cash payments to TANF mothers who marry, or, as in West Virginia, $100 monthly bonuses for TANF families in which parents are married.

In addition, states may use TANF funds for programs that advocate marriage. Hence, Arizona, for example, allocates 2.9 million TANF dollars to promote marriage, with $1 million reserved for "marriage and communication skills programs," $75,000 for vouchers for low-income married or cohabiting parents to pay for attending those marriage skills training courses, and $75,000 for development of a marriage handbook. Oklahoma plans to earmark 10 percent of TANF surplus funds to finance its Marriage Initiative, which will educate the public about the virtues of marriage and also make pro-marriage activities part of social service provision. In February 2001, Utah earmarked $600,000 of its TANF surplus funds for marriage education and formed a Marriage Commission. Wisconsin's TANF plan includes a "Community Marriage Policy" to be directed by a coordinator paid for with TANF dollars. [31] To reward states for their marriage initiatives and to encourage other states to follow suit, the Clinton administration announced a $10 million "high performance bonus" for the ten states with the largest increase in the percent of children living with married parents.[32]

Not to be outdone by administrative initiatives, congressmembers and welfare reform advocates have been contemplating ways to strengthen and expand fatherhood and marriage programs legislatively. Discussed primarily in terms of promoting "responsible fatherhood," congressional policy proposals would radically augment TANF's emphasis on the financial obligations of fathers—through child support—by equating marital, or at least residential, fatherhood with paternal responsibility. Such proposals have been espoused in various ideological quarters: by both Al Gore and George W. Bush during the 2000 presidential campaign, by moderate Republican congresswoman Nancy Johnson (R-Connecticut) and New Democratic senator Evan Bayh (D-Indiana), by the right wing Heritage Foundation's Robert Rector and progressive House Democrat Jesse Jackson, Jr. (D-Illinois).

The most extreme calls for marriage promotion and fatherhood enhancement come, not surprisingly, from Robert Rector and others at the Heritage Foundation and from Wade Horn, a founder of the National Fatherhood Initiative whom the second George Bush picked to become assistant secretary of the Department of Health and Human Services for welfare and related issues. In the Heritage Foundation's *Priorities for the President*, published to greet the new Bush presidency in January 2001, Rector proposed replacing the current financial incentives to states that increase their marriage rates with financial punishments to states that fail to do so. In addition, he urged policymakers to set aside $1 billion in TANF funds annually for marriage promotion activities, to offer incentives and rewards to parents who marry, and to create an affirmative action program in public housing for married couples.[33]

Many of Wade Horn's proposals closely track Rector's. Horn, whose confirmation as the Bush administration's welfare chief sailed through the Senate on a lopsided voice vote, has urged Congress to require states to promote marriage as a condition of participating in the TANF program, to make it clear that "neither cohabitation nor visitation is the equivalent of marriage," and to implement marriage incentives such as cash bonuses to welfare mothers who marry the child's biological father.[34] Horn also has endorsed Rector's suggestion that women "at high risk of bearing a child out of wedlock" be paid $1,000 annually for five years if they bear their first child within marriage and stay married.[35] In addition, he would further ratchet up the pressure on poor mothers to marry by limiting social programs—such as Head Start, public housing, and welfare—to married parents, allowing participation by single mothers only if funds are left over.[36]

Although the most strident calls to condition social benefits on poor mothers' family formation decisions come from conservatives, the idea that social policy should encourage marriage and promote fatherhood enjoys favor in both political parties. The first major fatherhood bill to surface in Congress was the Fathers Count Act, which breezed through the House of Representatives in fall 1999 with resoundingly bipartisan support (328–93).[37] During the final months of the 106th Congress in 2000, Representative Nancy Johnson, the bill's original sponsor, again shepherded fatherhood legislation through the House. The measure received thundering bipartisan approval in a vote of 405–18.[38] Part of the Child Support Distribution Act of 2000,[39] Johnson's bill included a $140 million matching grant program for local projects that promote marital family formation among poor single mothers and a $5 million award to a national fatherhood organization with "extensive experience in using married couples to deliver their program in the inner city."[40] The committee report accompanying the bill explained that "increasing the number and percentage of American children living in two-parent families is vital if the nation is to make serious and permanent progress against poverty."[41]

Pinning poverty reduction to the presence of a father's income, measures like the Johnson bill explicitly give fathers incentives to enter poor mothers' families. For example, the Johnson bill offered funds to projects that instruct fathers about their visitation and access rights,[42] forgave child support arrearages owed by men who become residential fathers, enhanced fathers' earning power through job training and "career-advancing education," and tracked non-marital fathers into various social services that encourage marriage.[43]

The problem with these proposals is not that they aim to support fathers, but that they do so at the expense of and without regard to the rights of mothers. Most mothers appreciate fathers' positive involvement with children, but not all mothers consider marital, residential fatherhood to be the sine qua non of such involvement.[44] Some mothers want fathers to nurture and mentor their children, but don't want to be on intimate terms with them. Some mothers do not want to confer social and emotional power on fathers merely because of a genetic tie. Others do not want legal impositions to undermine or demoralize social and emotional relations between fathers and children that already exist. Still others have expressly arranged or contracted to parent independently of biological fathers in co-parenting relationships with other women.

In addition to cheating mothers of the right to form families on their own terms, fatherhood proposals straitjacket mothers in the role of economic dependent. Even the more benign proposals, which include laudable provisions for job training and education for fathers, injure mothers by discriminating against them. Job training and education for mothers under TANF is erratic, limited, and hardly "career-advancing." A June 2001 study in Washington, D.C., showed, in fact, that of forty-three TANF recipients who showed up at job centers, *only one* received training.[45] Rather than fight poverty by improving economic opportunities for both sexes, fatherhood jobs programs revive the traditional focus on male breadwinners and mothers' dependence on them.

Although fatherhood proposals do not harm mothers directly, they structure mothers' choices, impair their independence, and undermine equity in mother-father relations. Imagine, for example, the pressure on a mother to permit her child's biological father to move in with them if that would mean he could escape his child support debts or avoid criminal penalties for defaulting on them. Or imagine the pressure on a mother to stay in an unwanted relationship with her child's father because social policy designates him to be the biological family's breadwinner.

The bipartisan appeal of fatherhood legislation cannot be understated; nor can its threat to women's right to mother independently. Progressive congressmember Jesse Jackson, Jr., for example, introduced a "Responsible Fatherhood" bill that duplicated the Johnson bill in many respects. The Jackson bill did not simply gesture to fathers; it disdained single mothers by describing them as dangers to their own children. Astoundingly, Jackson's bill repeated much of the race-coded, anti-single-mother rhetoric that had prefaced the Republicans' Personal Responsibility Act in 1996. For example, Jackson's bill asserted that "violent criminals are overwhelmingly males who grew up without fathers and the best predictor of crime in a community is the percentage of absent father households." It continued, "States should be encouraged, not restricted, from implementing programs that provide support for responsible fatherhood, promote marriage, and increase the incidence of marriage."[46]

The legislative campaign to promote fatherhood and marriage is not likely soon to wane. Four bipartisan fatherhood bills had been introduced into the 107th Congress by summer 2001, with at least one bill under serious consideration in each house. In the House of Representatives, Nancy Johnson's Child Support Distribution Act is back on the table, with its provisions for patriarchal family formation intact.[47] In the Senate, Evan Bayh (D-Indiana) and Olympia Snowe (R-Maine) have introduced the Strengthening Working Families Act, which mirrors the Johnson bill in promoting married fatherhood.[48] In addition, Evan Bayh has introduced the Responsible Fatherhood Act of 2001, which enjoys support from members of the progressive Congressional Black Caucus.[49] The bill stresses marriage even more than did previous versions, through provisions that would require fatherhood programs to promote marriage through counseling, mentoring, dissemination of pro-marriage information to encourage fathers to choose marriage, as well as through similar initiatives designed to convince parents to stay married.[50]

These bipartisan marriage and fatherhood initiatives assume that poor mothers' decisions about family forms and relationships cause their poverty. They also assume that it is appropriate for government to interfere in the intimate associational life of poor mothers. Even as government scales back its affirmative role in mitigating poverty, it is intensifying its coercive reach into the lives of the poor. Now squarely at the center of the poverty debate, marriage promotion and fatherhood initiatives seek to compel mothers to follow the government's moral prescriptions and to accept economic dependence on men.

It is true that a family with a male wage earner generally is better off than a family without one. While some moralistic welfare strategists believe that married fatherhood per se is an important governmental objective, more pragmatic policy strategists argue syllogistically that if men's families are better off economically than women's, then poverty can be cured by the presence of a breadwinning man in every family.[51] This kind of thinking short-circuits equality, foreclosing the question of improving women's own income.

If we look at the various measures of women's and mothers' poverty—women's income as compared to men's, for example—it is clear that single mothers are poor because women's work is not valued. This is true of women's labor market work, where a racialized gender gap in wages reflects the devaluation of the work women do, especially when women of color do it. And it is also true of women's nonmarket care-giving work, which garners no income at all.

## Ensuring Independence

In 2002, under the terms of the 1996 PRA, the block grants that fund the TANF program expire. This means that the TANF program will have to be reauthorized. The reauthorization process presents an opportunity to change the terms of TANF— one way or another. At this writing, proposals to strengthen TANF's provisions for patriarchal family formation are the main game in town. Even so, some feminist groups (e.g., NOW-Legal Defense and Education Fund and the Women's Committee of 100), some welfare rights groups (e.g., the Welfare Made A Difference Campaign), and some low-income community groups (e.g., the National Campaign for Jobs and Income Support) have been working valiantly to shift the debate toward the economic issues that must be faced so that we can make welfare's end the end of poverty.

As a first step toward ending poverty, we must recognize that single mothers' poverty arises inexorably from the fact that women's care-giving work for their own families is not accorded economic value. The interconnectedness between poverty and unremunerated care-giving never has received wide or focused political attention in the United States. Most labor union and other social justice organizing, for example, has focused on improving the pay and conditions of wage work, beginning with the historical trade union emphasis on the (male) family wage. Most U.S. feminists, meanwhile, have been leery of taking up the cause of women's care-giving work in their own families, preferring to promote women's equality among wage workers than to risk a return to compulsory domesticity.

In response to the TANF regime, however, some feminists have begun not only to resist welfare's moral discipline but also to argue that we should reconceive welfare as a care-givers' income.[52] As such, welfare would assist care-givers *because of what they do* rather than in spite of what they don't do—because what care-givers do for their families is *work*. Moreover, it is work that is indispensable not only to a care-giver's (usually a mother's) own family, but to her community, the economy, and the polity, as well.

If we can adjust our frame theoretically and politically to see that care-giving *is* work, we can begin to understand the impossible position poor single mothers find themselves in when unforgiving social policy tells them that because they are not married, they must perform two full-time jobs. We all know that family work—household management and parenting—takes skill, energy, time, and responsibility. We know this because people who can afford it *pay* other people to do such work. Many wage-earning mothers pay for child care; upper-class mothers who work outside the home pay for nannies; very wealthy mothers who don't work outside the home pay household workers to assist them with their various tasks. Moreover, even when we are not paying surrogates to do our family care-giving, we pay people to perform activities in the labor market that care-givers also do in the home. We pay drivers—bus drivers, taxi drivers, limousine drivers—to take us places; we pay nurses to make us feel better and help us get well; we pay psychologists to help us with our troubles; we pay teachers to explain our lessons; we pay cooks and waitresses to prepare and serve our food.

If economists can measure the value of this work when it is performed for other people's families, why can't we impute value to it when it is performed for one's own? In 1972, economists at the Chase Manhattan Bank did just that, translating family care-giving work into its labor market components—nursemaid, dietitian, cook, laundress, maintenance man, chauffeur, food buyer, cook, dishwasher, seamstress, practical nurse, gardener. They concluded that the weekly value of family care-givers' work was at least $257.53, or $13,391.56 a year (1972 dollars).[53] Had poor single mothers received comparable welfare benefits in 1996 they would have had incomes above the poverty line. Had these benefits explicitly compensated them for the work they do, poor single mothers would not have had to live under the stigma of "welfare dependency."

If we think about welfare as an indemnity for family care-giving work that *someone* has to do, we can see that there is no need to end it. Instead, we should redefine welfare as an income owed to nonmarket, care-giving workers—owed to anyone who bears sole or primary responsibility for children (or for other dependent family members). Following the survivors' insurance system of regular and unconditional benefits for eligible participants, this income should be nationally guaranteed and paid automatically to care-givers because of the work they do, not because of who they are or what their families look like. And following the survivors' insurance system of support for care-givers when they negotiate a balance between care-giving and wage-earning, this income should be portable and transferable, meaning that care-givers should be able to use it to purchase surrogate care if they choose to work in the labor market. But more redistributive than survivors' insurance because conceived where poverty and care-giving intersect, this income should taper off as family incomes surpass living wages.

A care-givers' income would relieve the disproportionate burdens that fall on single mothers and in so doing would lessen inequalities among women based on class, race, and marital status, and between male and female parents based on conventional social roles. Although provided primarily to attenuate the compounded burdens of the care-giver who is parenting alone, this income should also be available to low-income sexual and kinship families of more than one adult so that co-parents can negotiate whether and how to share care-giving and wage-earning. This would attenuate the assumption that the need for welfare is a measure of deficient family structure: all families with incomes below, say, 300 percent of the poverty threshold would be eligible to receive it. (In 2000, the poverty threshold for a family of three with two children was $13,374.)[54] It would also attenuate the strict gender division of labor in heterosexual families with more than one adult: mothers and fathers could share care-giving without sacrificing income support. But most important, it would recognize and honor care-givers as independent citizens whose care-giving work is an aspect of citizenship, not a distraction from it.

A care-givers' income would also provide a conceptual basis for incorporating all care-givers into the Social Security system as workers entitled to their own benefits. Under the current system, a full-time care-giver's Social Security benefits are derived from and are less than her wage-earning spouse's entitlement. In a welfare state that treated care-giving work and wage work equitably, a family care-giver would receive retirement benefits based on her own contributions to society, not her husband's. Accordingly all care-givers would become eligible for Social Security, not just those who are married. Wage-earning women (and sometimes men) who are currently penalized by the Social Security system when they leave the labor market temporarily to care for children or other dependents would be credited for their work as care-givers, thus improving their benefit levels. In addition, the wage-earning survivor of a deceased care-giver would be entitled to receive survivors' insurance benefits, and thus to decide how to meet his new responsibilities as his children's sole care-giver.

We need to redefine welfare in this way to enable equality— between the sexes, among women, in spite of poverty, and under the Constitution. Income support for all care-givers who are going it alone would permit them to decide how best to manage their responsibilities to children and would affirm their right to do so. Offering an income to all care-givers in a unitary system based on income, not family structure—to non-marital mothers as well as to married or widowed ones—would erase invidious moral distinctions among mothers and eliminate their racial effects. This would promote equality among women—especially between middle-class married care-givers who enjoy social and political support when they choose to work in the home raising children and poor unmarried care-givers whom welfare policy now compels to choose wages over children.

A care-givers' income might even help undermine the sexual division of labor, as well, for some men might be enticed to do family care-giving work once they understood it to have economic value. Further, income support for co-parent families that are struggling to make ends meet would permit care-givers in parental relationships to retain economic means and personal independence even when care-giving time steals from wages. Finally, providing care-givers with economic means in their own right would promote equality in father-mother relations by enabling mothers to choose to stay with fathers because they want to, not because they have to—or to leave unhappy, subordinating, or violent relationships with them. In these ways and more, a care-givers' income would restore constitutional rights that the current welfare system either threatens or has taken away—rights that are foundational to personhood and independence.

Remuneration for the care-giving work performed mostly by mothers is not a panacea for mothers' poverty or inequality, of course. It would not immunize them from government's interference in their lives, for example. But it would raise the threshold for such interference. Where government now regulates recipients' intimate associations as a condition of cash assistance, the only condition government could reasonably impose on a care-givers' income would be whether the labor was, in fact, done. A care-givers' income would not depend on a mother's (or father's) private moral choices or cultural practices—would not depend on *how* the job was done but on *whether* it was done. The fundamental right to parent would insulate recipients from meddling by government; this right establishes the presumption that the care-giver *does* do her job, and a long line of cases has established that she may do her job as she deems appropriate. The right to parent would shield care-givers from intrusion by requiring government to establish a compelling justification—child abuse or abandonment, for example—to override the rights of parents.

Redefining welfare this way will remedy inequality where it is most gendered—in the care-giving relations of social reproduction. Yet it will not be enough to end welfare by replacing it with a care-givers' income. The end of welfare—the goal of feminist social policy—must be to enhance the full spectrum of choices for all women. We need to improve women's opportunities as *both* nonmarket and market workers, so that a care-giver's choice to work in the home is backed up by the possibility of choosing not to. Toward that end, we must enable care-giving mothers to voluntarily receive education, training, and assistance in job placement. Enriched options in the labor market will enrich the choice to work inside the home; they will also prepare care-givers to choose not to work inside the home once the need for full-time care-giving work has ended. We must also win labor market reforms that will make outside work feasible even for mothers who are parenting alone. Unless we make outside work affordable for solo care-givers, a care-givers' income would constrain choice by favoring care-giving over wage-earning. And, unless we make outside work equitable and rewarding for all women, a caregivers' income would deter equality by discouraging women's choice *not* to care.

The end of welfare, then, includes "making work pay" not only by remunerating care-giving work but also by improving the opportunities, working conditions, compensation, and social supports associated with wage-earning. This will require vigorous enforcement of antidiscrimination laws; a living wage; comparable worth policies; a full employment policy; massive investment in education, job training, and skills enhancement—

in addition to policies that attend to the care needs of dependent children and elderly or disabled adult family members.

## Reforming Welfare Reform

Given the long history of racism and stigma in welfare politics, we are not likely soon to win a caregivers' income. Nor—given conservative control of the White House, House of Representatives, and Supreme Court—are we likely soon to win the dramatic labor market policies necessary to end the workplace subordination of people of color and white women. But we might be able to reform welfare reform to redirect welfare policy toward mitigating and reducing the poverty of mothers and their children. If we change welfare's end in this way, we can begin to restore mothers' rights under TANF. Once poor mothers begin to recover their citizenship, we can begin to expand the terms of citizenship to include the material supports due to family care-givers.

The reauthorization of TANF in 2002 presents an opportunity to repeal provisions that injure mothers and to add provisions that promote economic security. Under discussion among progressives in Congress as well as among grassroots and advocacy groups are proposals to amend TANF in ten fundamental ways:[55]

(1) Redefine the statutory purposes of TANF to be (a) the provision of assistance to families in need so that children can be raised in their own homes and (b) the reduction of poverty. Strike the current goal of promoting marital, father-mother family formation.

(2) Expand the concept of "work activity." Education and job training at all levels and of any duration should count toward meeting TANF's work requirement. A parent's full-

time at-home care-giving for children under age six also should count as a work activity, as should at-home care of a sick or disabled child of any age. In addition, part-time care-giving for children over six who lack adequate after-school care or supervision should satisfy the work requirement.

(3) To attenuate time limits, stop the clock for families receiving TANF that are in compliance with program rules. This would assist many families, including those in which a parent is in school or job training or is providing at-home care for a child under age six, as both activities would satisfy the revised work requirement.

(4) End draconian punishments by prohibiting full family sanctions. Instead of permitting states to kick whole families out of TANF when a mother doesn't meet a stipulation, require states to reduce the family benefit only incrementally, based on the mother's share.

(5) Restore the constitutionally guaranteed privacy and intimate associational rights of poor mothers by making paternity establishment and child support cooperation voluntary for mothers. As an incentive to voluntary participation in these programs, designate mothers, not government, the recipient of child support payments.

(6) Assure the safety interests of families enrolled in TANF by making various requirements more flexible for families dealing with domestic or intimate violence. The current Family Violence Option should become a requirement for states.

(7) Protect all children in poor families by prohibiting the "family cap." Guarantee benefits to all children in a TANF family, whether or not a child was born while her mother was enrolled in TANF.

(8) End the "illegitimacy bonus," which rewards states that decrease non-marital birthrates the most. The bonus gives incentive to states to interfere with women's marital and re-

productive decisions. Replace it with a poverty reduction bonus to reward states that lower poverty rates the most.

(9) Assure children that their care needs will be met when parents enter the labor market. Restore the child care entitlement for TANF families.

(10) Vigorously and rigorously enforce all antidiscrimination and labor standards laws within the TANF regime. This includes enforcing the minimum wage guarantee for all TANF participants who engage in paid or unpaid labor market work. It also includes enforcing Civil Rights Act prohibitions on race discrimination (Title VI and Title VII) as well as Title VII and Title IX prohibitions on sex discrimination.

These reforms will not end TANF; they will only attenuate the terms of participating in it. Still, changing the terms of TANF will open opportunities (e.g., education and training); reward all forms of work (including at-home care-giving); return fundamental rights (reproductive, parental, associational, vocational); and assure equal protection in its broadest sense, by guarding the safety of families and providing for the care needs of children in poverty. So reformed, TANF will provide basic economic security for poor families as we pursue an agenda to end women's poverty and ensure women's equality by rewarding women's work wherever it is performed.

# Notes

## Chapter 1. Welfare as a Condition of Women's Equality

1. Senator Daniel Patrick Moynihan (D-New York), quoted in Robert Pear, "Senate Votes to Deny Benefits to Legal Aliens," *New York Times*, July 20, 1996, p. 9; Robert Pear, "Senate Approves Sweeping Change in Welfare Policy," *New York Times*, July 24, 1996, p. 1.

2. During the 1995 debate the Democrats unanimously endorsed the Deal substitute, which imposed work requirements and time limits but preserved the welfare entitlement for individuals. This proposal was offered by then-Democrat Nathan Deal of Georgia, who became a Republican shortly thereafter.

3. See the full text of the Castle-Tanner substitute amendment to HR3734 in the *Congressional Record*, July 18, 1996, pp. H7907-7974. P.L. 104-193, Title I, part A, section 401(b) stipulates "No Individual Entitlement." Section 408(a-2) provides "no additional cash assistance for children born to families receiving assistance." Section 408(a-3) reduces or ends assistance to families where the mother does not comply with paternity establishment and child support enforcement requirements. Title III, section I encourages states to establish both mandatory and voluntary programs to enhance fathers' access to their children.

4. William Goodling (R-Pennsylvania) in the *Congressional Record*, July 18, 1996, p. H7975.

5. *Congressional Record*, July 18, 1996, pp. H7974-H7975, H7981-

H7982, H7985, S8123-8126; Daniel Patrick Moynihan quoted in Robert Pear, "Senate Votes to Deny Benefits to Legal Aliens"; Jason DeParle, "Get a Job: The New Contract with America's Poor," *New York Times*, July 28, 1996, section 4, p. 1.

6. *Congressional Record*, July 19, 1996, p. S8330.

7. Under waivers to the Family Support Act of 1988, twenty-two states had imposed time limits on welfare eligibility by late 1995. Sam Howe Verhovek, "States Are Already Providing Glimpse at Welfare's Future," *New York Times*, September 21, 1995, p. 1. Twenty states had taken steps to impose the family cap (no additional benefits provided to children born to women on welfare). Barbara Vobejda, "Most States Are Shaping Their Own Welfare Reform," *Washington Post*, February 3, 1996, p.1.

8. The Supreme Court first extended rights to welfare recipients beginning in 1968. See *King v. Smith* 392 U.S. 309 (1968), striking down Alabama's "substitute father" rule denying welfare payments to the children of a mother who "cohabits" in or outside her home with any single or married able-bodied man. The Court found that moralistic state eligibility criteria interfered with the statutory purpose of AFDC. See also *New Jersey Welfare Rights Organization et al. v. Cahill*, per curiam (1973), striking down New Jersey's statute limiting benefits to households in which the parents are "ceremonially married."

9. The right to marry was recognized as a core due process liberty in *Meyer v. Nebraska* 262 U.S. 390 (1923). Beginning in the 1970s, decisions about marriage were included among those personal decisions protected by the right to privacy. *Carey v. Population Services International* 431 U.S. 678 (1977); *Zablocki v. Redhail* 434 U.S. 374 (1978). See also *Skinner v. Oklahoma* 316 U.S. 535 (1942), stating that "marriage is one of the 'basic civil rights of man,'" and *Loving v. Virginia* 388 U.S. 1 (1967). On the right to care for one's own children, see, e.g., *May v. Anderson* 345 U.S. 528 (1953), and *Stanley v. Illinois* 405 U.S. 645 (1972). On procreative liberty, see *Skinner, Carey, Roe v. Wade* 410 U.S. 113 (1973), and *Planned Parenthood of Southeastern Pennsylvania v. Casey* 112 S. Ct. 2791 (1992).

10. The Supreme Court has interpreted the Thirteenth Amendment narrowly. Still, in the early twentieth-century Peonage Cases, the Court established the principle that coerced employment in satis-

faction of a debt is involuntary servitude; and in *United States v. Kozminski* 487 U.S. 931 (1988), the Court found that "involuntary servitude is a condition in which the victim is forced to work by the use or threat of physical or legal coercion." Cynthia Bailey, "Workfare and Involuntary Servitude—What You Wanted to Know but Were Afraid to Ask," *Boston College Third World Law Journal* 15 (Summer 1995): 292–96.

11. E.g., Women's Committee of One Hundred, "Why Every Woman in America Should Beware of Welfare Cuts," *New York Times*, August 8, 1995 (full-page ad).

12. Felicia Kornbluh, "Feminists and the Welfare Debate: Too Little? Too Late?" *dollars and sense*, November/December 1996, p. 25.

13. Jane Goodman, Elizabeth F. Loftus, Marian Miller, and Edith Greene, "Money, Sex, and Death: Gender Bias in Wrongful Death Damage Awards," *Law and Society Review* 25 (1991): 263–85.

14. *Dred Scott v. Sandford* 19 How. (60 U.S.) 393 (1857).

15. *Minor v. Happersett* 88 U.S. 162, 11 L.Ed. 627 (1875).

16. *Palko v. Connecticut* 302 U.S. 319 (1937) discussed the scheme of fundamental rights and asked of governmental action, "Does it violate those fundamental principles of liberty and justice which lie at the base of all our civil and political institutions?"

17. *United States v. Carolene Products* 304 U.S. 144 (1938), note 4, planted the seed for modern Fourteenth Amendment jurisprudence. In this footnote, Justice Harlan Stone suggested that courts might apply special scrutiny in cases affecting fundamental rights or where legislation singles out racial, national, or religious minorities.

18. *Bolling v. Sharpe* 347 U.S. 497 (1954).

19. *Loving v. Virginia* 388 U.S. 1 (1967) found that "under our Constitution, the freedom to marry, or not marry . . . resides with the individual and cannot be infringed by the State." *Skinner v. Oklahoma* 316 U.S. 535 struck down the compulsory sterilization of certain classes of felons as a discriminatory violation of "the right to have offspring." *Planned Parenthood of Southeastern Pennsylvania v. Casey* 112 S. Ct. 2791 (1992) upheld a woman's right to terminate pregnancy as an aspect of her right to chart her own destiny and make her own place in society.

20. *Gideon v. Wainwright* 372 U.S. 335 (1963).

21. Theodore J. Lowi, conversation with author.

22. *Flemming v. Nestor* 363 U.S. 603, 608–609 (1960); *Weinberger v. Wiesenfeld* 420 U.S. 636 (1975).
23. Robert D. Hershey, Jr., "Misunderstanding Social Security," *New York Times,* August 20, 1995.
24. See, e.g., *Jefferson v. Hackney* 406 U.S. 535, 575 (1972). Justice Thurgood Marshall noted in his dissent that Texas had funded welfare at a lower level than other social benefits because it is politically unpopular, because a stigma uniquely attaches to welfare recipients, and because a large proportion of welfare recipients are people of color.
25. In 1993, the average monthly benefit for a widowed mother was $448, and for each surviving child, $443, subject to a family benefit limit. Where the spouse died at age forty and had earned the national average wage, the monthly family benefit limit was $1,527. U. S. House of Representatives, Committee on Ways and Means, *1994 Green Book: Overview of Entitlement Programs* (Washington, D.C., 1994), pp. 4, 37. A wage earner insured under the social security system who died at age forty in 1995 left his widow and children a maximum family benefit of $1,362 per month if he earned $20,000 annually. See Congressional Research Service, *1995 Guide to Social Security and Medicare* (Washington, D.C., 1994), p. 30; Social Security Administration, *Social Security Handbook,* 12th ed. (Washington, D.C., 1995). The average monthly welfare benefit in 1993 was $367.
26. *King v. Smith* stated that welfare must be provided to all eligible persons (see note 8, above).
27. *Shapiro v. Thompson* 394 U.S. 618 (1969) held that Connecticut's residency requirements were unconstitutional discrimination and violated the right to travel; *Goldberg v. Kelly* 397 U.S. 254 (1970) found welfare a "statutory entitlement," triggering due process protections for recipients in their relations with welfare agencies.
28. *Dandridge v. Williams* 397 U.S. 471 (1970) upheld Maryland's family benefit limit and thus rejected the claim that individuals have a right to a particular or equal amount of cash payment. "Toughlove Index," *New York Times,* December 8, 1996.
29. See Kathleen M. Sullivan, "Unconstitutional Conditions," *Harvard Law Review* 102, no. 7 (May 1989): 1413–1506. On welfare reform and reproductive liberty, see Catherine R. Albiston and Laura Beth Nielsen, "Welfare Queens and Other Fairy Tales: Wel-

fare Reform and Unconstitutional Reproductive Controls,"
*Howard Law Journal* 38, no. 3 (Summer 1995): 473–519.

30. In addition to probable rights violations contained in the new
welfare policy is its questionable claim of a federal police power
governing family matters. See *United States v. Lopez* 115 S. Ct. 1624
(1995), narrowly tying Congress's power to regulate to those activities that directly affect interstate commerce and "withholding
from Congress a plenary police power." The Court rejected the
federal government's "national productivity" reasoning, according to which "Congress could regulate any activity that it found
was related to the economic productivity of individual citizens:
family law (including marriage, divorce, and child custody), for
example"; the Court argued further that "if we were to accept the
Government's arguments, we are hard-pressed to posit any
activity by an individual that Congress is without power to
regulate."

31. *Harris v. McRae* 448 U.S. 297 (1980).

32. *Webster v. Reproductive Health Services* 492 U.S. 490, 507 (1989),
reiterated in *Rust v. Sullivan* 500 U.S. 173, 201 (1991).

33. Robin West, *Progressive Constitutionalism* (Durham, N.C., 1994)
especially chapters 1–3, discovers affirmative guarantees in the
Fourteenth Amendment from its legislative history and argues that
Congress has broad responsibilities to enforce those guarantees.

34. *Planned Parenthood of Southeastern Pennsylvania v. Casey* 112 S. Ct.
2791 (1992).

35. Sex classifications may be used to compensate women "for particular economic disabilities [they have] suffered" (*Califano v.
Webster* 430 U.S. 313, 320 [1977]) and to "promote equal employment opportunity" (*California Federal Savings & Loan Association v.
Guerra* 479 U.S. 272, 289 [1987]).

36. Justice Thurgood Marshall for the Court, quoting from a sponsor
of the Pregnancy Discrimination Act, *CalFed v. Guerra,* 289.

37. *United States v. Virginia et al.* no. 94–1941 (1996).

38. In some places as many as 60–80 percent of welfare recipients are
or have been victims of domestic violence as adults. NOW–LDEF
Fact Sheet, "The Safety Net Saves Lives," December 1995. See also
Martha F. Davis and Susan J. Kraham, "Protecting Women's Welfare in the Face of Violence," *Fordham Urban Law Journal* 22 (Summer 1995): 1141–57.

39. I discuss these issues at length in *The Wages of Motherhood: Inequality in the Welfare State, 1917–1942* (Ithaca, N.Y., 1995).

40. President Bill Clinton, announcing his decision to sign the Personal Responsibility Act, Cable News Network (CNN), July 31, 1996. Transcript issued by the Office of the Press Secretary, the White House.

41. On procreation in welfare politics and policy, see Linda C. McClain, "'Irresponsible' Reproduction," *Hastings Law Journal* 47, no. 2 (January 1996): 339–453.

42. Lyndon Johnson to his budget director, White House telephone tapes, CNN Morning News, October 18, 1996.

43. Dorothy Roberts, "The Value of Black Mothers' Work," *Connecticut Law Review* 26 (Spring 1994): 871–73; Lucy A. Williams, "Race, Rat Bites, and Unfit Mothers: How Media Discourse Informs Welfare Legislation Debate," *Fordham Urban Law Journal* 22 (1995): 1159–96.

44. The primary authors of these three principal strands of punitive welfare thought are Lawrence Mead (*The New Politics of Poverty* [New York, 1992]) who prescribes work to improve the character of the needy; Charles Murray (*Losing Ground: American Social Policy, 1950–1980* [New York, 1984]) who calls for negative incentives to reduce non-marital births which reproduce the needy; and Marvin Olasky (*The Tragedy of American Compassion* [Lanham, Md., 1992]) who sees destitution as an opportunity to spiritually awaken the needy. See Adam Wolfson, "Welfare Fixers," *Commentary* 101 (April 1996): 38–41.

45. "Sign It," *The New Republic*, August 12, 1996, p. 8.

46. U. S. House of Representatives, C-SPAN, March 23, 1995.

47. Ann Crittenden Scott, "The Value of Housework: For Love or Money?" *Ms.*, July 1972, 56–59; John Kenneth Galbraith, "How the Economy Hangs on Her Apron Strings," *Ms.*, May 1974, 74–77.

48. This position was most famously developed by Marianosa Dalla Costa (with Selma James) in "The Power of Women and the Subversion of the Community," *Radical America* 6 (1972): 67–102.

49. On the labor market focus of feminist thinking about women's poverty, see Barbara Bergmann and Heidi Hartmann, "A Welfare Reform Based on Help for Working Parents," *Feminist Economics* 1 (Summer 1995): 85–91.

50. Actually, this is not just an assumption. Even before enactment of the Personal Responsibility Act, the state of Virginia, for example, encouraged welfare mothers to become child care providers for other welfare mothers. The PRA defines child care services performed by a recipient for another recipient as "work" if the latter recipient is engaged in mandatory community service. P.L. 104-193, Title I, section 407(d)(12).

51. U.S. General Accounting Office, *Mother-Only Families: Low Earnings Will Keep Many Children in Poverty* (Washington, D.C., 1991), pp. 6–8, 24–25. According to this study, 70 percent of poor single mothers who work thirty hours per week receive gross income below the poverty line. Thirty-five percent of poor single mothers who work forty hours per week live below the poverty line; after paying for child care, 55 percent of full-time, wage-earning poor single mothers live in poverty. The best-case scenarios predict that poor single mothers will work less than full-time (between thirty and forty hours per week) because of child-rearing responsibilities. Of poor single mothers who work, say, thirty-five hours per week, 55 percent live below the poverty line based on gross income and seventy percent live in poverty after paying for child care.

52. *United States v. Kozminski* 487 U.S. 931, 942, 952 (1988). See note 10. The Court held "that in every case in which [it] . . . found a condition of involuntary servitude, the victim had no available choice but to work or be subject to legal sanction. . . . The term 'involuntary servitude' necessarily means a condition of servitude in which the victim is forced to work for the defendant by the use or threat of physical restraint or physcial injury, or by the use or threat of coercion through law or the legal process. This definition encompasses those cases in which the defendant holds the victim in servitude by placing the victim in fear of such physical restraint or injury or legal coercion."

53. The IRAs-for-homemakers provision was part of the Small Business Job Protection and Minimum Wage Increase bill, H.R. 3448.

54. *Congressional Record,* August 2, 1996, p. H9847.

55. P.L. 104-193, Title I, section 407(d)(12).

56. Ibid., Title I, section 408(a)(2); Title III, subtitle D, section 333.

57. Ibid., Title I, section 407(a)(2).

58. *Skinner v. Oklahoma,* note 9 above.

59. See *May v. Anderson* 345 U.S. 528, 533 (1953); *Stanley v. Illinois* 405 U.S. 645 (1972); *Santosky v. Kramer* 455 U.S. 745, 758–759 (1982). *Meyer v. Nebraska* 262 U.S. 390, 399 (1923) recognizes the right to "establish a home and bring up children" as an element of due process liberty. See also *Weinberger v. Wiesenfeld* 420 U.S. 636, 651 (1975), citing the parent's right to care for her / his child as a reason to include fathers in the survivors' insurance system, "given [its] purpose of enabling the surviving parent to remain at home to care for a child."

60. *M.L.B. v. S.L.J.* S.Ct. no. 95-853 (December 16, 1996).

61. *Stanley v. Illinois* 65, quoting *Kovacs v. Cooper* 336 U.S. 77, 95 (1949).

62. *Pierce v. Society of Sisters* 268 U.S. 510, 534 (1925).

## Chapter 2. How We Got Welfare Reform

1. U. S. Department of Health and Human Services, Administration for Children and Families, Office of Family Assistance, *Characteristics and Financial Circumstances of AFDC Recipients, FY 1991* (Washington, D.C., 1991), table 6; Congressional Research Service, March 22, 1994.

2. Heidi Hartmann, Roberta Spalter-Roth, and Jacqueline Chu, "Poverty Alleviation and Single-mother Families," *Phi Kappa Phi Journal* (Summer 1996): 25; Kathleen Mullan Harris, "Work and Welfare among Single Mothers in Poverty," *American Journal of Sociology* 99 (1993): 317–52.

3. David Whitman, "Was It Good for Us?" *U.S. News and World Report,* May 19, 1997, pp. 56–64.

4. The Court so described the shift in the policy of Aid to Families with Dependent Children (AFDC) that began with the Social Security Act Amendments of 1967. *New York Department of Social Services v. Dublino* 413 U.S. 405, 412 (1972).

5. Quoted in Winifred Bell, *Aid to Dependent Children* (New York, 1965), p. 68.

6. James T. Patterson, *America's Struggle against Poverty, 1900–1980* (Cambridge, Mass., 1981), p. 88.

7. Blanche D. Coll, *Safety Net: Welfare and Social Security, 1929–1979* (New Brunswick, N.J., 1995), pp. 187–88.

8. Sandra Meucci, dissertation MS, chapter 2, University of California–Santa Cruz, quoting Julius Paul, "The Return of Punitive Sterilization Proposals," *Law and Society Review* 2 (1968).

9. Mark J. Stern discusses the 1994 Clinton welfare reform proposal as creating moral apartheid in "What We Talk about When We Talk about Welfare," *Tikkun* 9 (November–December 1994): 29–32.

10. Joanne Goodwin illuminates the place of wage-earning in welfare policy in "'Employable Mothers' and 'Suitable Work': A Re-evaluation of Welfare and Wage-earning for Women in the Twentieth-century United States," *Journal of Social History* 29 (Winter 1995): 253–75.

11. Joel F. Handler, *Reforming the Poor: Welfare Policy, Federalism, and Morality* (New York, 1972), p. 36.

12. Sarah A. Soule and Yvonne Zylan, "Runaway Train: The Diffusion of State-level Reform in AFDC Eligibility Requirements, 1940–1967," unpublished paper (1996).

13. Sonya Michel, "From Welfare to Workfare: The Paradigm Shifts of the 1960s," paper presented at the Social Science History Association annual meetings, 1995.

14. Quoted in Coll, *Safety Net*, p. 190.

15. The 1962 amendments created the AFDC–Unemployed Father program, though on an experimental basis. In 1967, the Congress made the program permanent. Under AFDC–UF, states were permitted to extend AFDC coverage to two-parent families where the father was unemployed. After the Supreme Court found the unemployed father program to be gender-biased in 1979 (*Califano v. Westcott* 99 S. Ct. 2655) AFDC–UF became AFDC–Unemployed Parent. The state option to participate in AFDC–UP became a requirement in 1988. AFDC–UP rules were not identical to those applicable to single-parent families. Among other things, they included time limits.

16. Handler, *Reforming the Poor*, p. 41; Sylvia Law, "Women, Work, Welfare, and the Preservation of Patriarchy," *University of Pennsylvania Law Review* 131 (May 1983): 1266.

17. Testimony of Assistant Secretary of Labor Jerome M. Rosow, U. S. House of Representatives, Committee on Ways and Means, *Hearings on Social Security and Welfare Proposals*, 91st Congress, 1st session (Washington, D.C., 1970), p. 384.

18. Daniel Patrick Moynihan, "How the Great Society 'destroyed the American family'," *The Public Interest* no. 108 (Summer 1992): 56, quoting from his September 1965 discussion of the Black family in the Jesuit journal *America*.

19. U. S. Department of Health, Education and Welfare secretary Elliot Richardson, quoted in Jill Quadagno, *The Color of Welfare* (New York, 1994), p. 127.

20. States did not match the federal investment in job training, education, and child care as the law required them to do. And such job training as did occur often pushed mothers into unstable, low-wage jobs.

21. *Congressional Record*, September 29, 1988, p. S13639.

22. Teresa Moore, "States Aren't Helping Poor Families Enough, Study Shows," *San Francisco Chronicle*, November 20, 1996.

23. Roger Gay, "A Brief History of Prevailing Child Support Doctrine," http://www.lectlaw.com/tfam.html, in Kids—Custody, Support, Etc. section (italics added).

24. 42 U.S.C. section 666.

25. The *Congressional Quarterly* observed: "In the sea of discord over welfare reform, there was one island of bipartisan consensus: provisions that significantly increased government involvement in forcing absent parents to support their children." *Congress and the Nation, Volume VII* (Washington, D.C., 1990), p. 617.

26. P.L. 104-193, Title I, part A (Block Grants to States for Temporary Assistance for Needy Families), section 401.

27. For a discussion of how punitive welfare provisions serve as incentives to marriage, see Douglas J. Besharov with Timothy S. Sullivan, "Welfare Reform and Marriage," *The Public Interest* no. 125 (Fall 1996): 94.

28. Legal immigrants who enter the U. S. from now on are barred from TANF benefits for at least five years. Thereafter, states may withhold TANF eligibility from noncitizen immigrants other than: asylees and refugees; veterans, soldiers and their spouses and dependent children; and noncitizen immigrants who have worked forty qualifying quarters as defined by the Social Security Act without using federal means-tested benefits. In other words, states have the option to disqualify most legal immigrants from cash assistance altogether. This applies to noncitizen immigrants' eligi-

bility for other federal means-tested benefits, as well—including Medicaid. P.L. 104-193, Title I, section 402(a)(1)(B)(ii) and Title IV, sections 401–403, 411–412.

29. P.L. 104-193, Title I, part A, sections 403, 404, 417. Section 417 states: "No officer or employee of the Federal Government may regulate the conduct of States under this part or enforce any provision of this part, except to the extent expressly provided in this part."

30. See my *Wages of Motherhood: Inequality in the Welfare State, 1917– 1942* (Ithaca, N.Y., 1995), chapter 2.

31. House and Senate committee reports on the Social Security Act of 1935 indicate that the states were free to impose moral conditions on eligibility.

32. A U. S. Children's Bureau study and others reported that unemployment rates were highest among Black women during the Depression, for example, and that larger numbers of African American mothers than white mothers parented alone. See my *Wages of Motherhood*, pp. 128, 140–41.

33. 42 U.S.C. section 402(g)(1). The Advisory Council on Social Security, which developed the survivors' insurance program, explained that widows' benefits were "intended as supplements to the orphans' benefits with the purpose of enabling the widow to remain at home and care for the children." Advisory Council on Social Security, *Final Report* (Washington, D.C., 1938). For a feminist history of this policy decision, see Alice Kessler-Harris, "Designing Women and Old Fools: The Construction of the Social Security Amendments of 1939," in Linda Kerber, Alice Kessler-Harris, and Kathryn Kish Sklar, eds., *U. S. History as Women's History* (Chapel Hill, N.C., 1995), pp. 87–106.

34. Racism continues to feed hostility to welfare. See Martin Gilens, "'Race Coding' and White Opposition to Welfare," *American Political Science Review* 90 (September 1996): 593–604, which finds that "whites' perceptions of blacks as lazy appear more important in shaping opposition to welfare than do their perceptions of poor people as lazy," and that "negative beliefs about black welfare mothers were associated with significantly more negative views of welfare in general than were negative beliefs about white welfare mothers" (pp. 598, 600).

35. Robert H. Mugge, "Aid to Families with Dependent Children: Initial Findings of the 1961 Report on the Characteristics of Recipients," *Social Security Bulletin* 23 (March 1963): 4.

36. Social Security Administration, Bureau of Public Assistance, *Illegitimacy and Its Impact on the Aid to Dependent Children Program* (Washington, D.C., 1960), p. 53.

37. Bell, *Aid to Dependent Children*, p. 137.

38. Quoted in *King v. Smith* 392 U.S. 309, 322, 323 (1968).

39. On the legal movement for welfare rights, see Martha F. Davis, *Brutal Need: Lawyers and the Welfare Rights Movement, 1960–1973* (New Haven, Conn., 1993). On the mobilization and development of recipients' welfare rights movement, see Guida West, *The National Welfare Rights Movement: The Social Protest of Poor Women* (New York, 1981) and Frances Fox Piven and Richard A. Cloward, *Poor Peoples' Movements: Why They Succeed, How They Fail* (New York, 1977), chapter 5.

40. R. Shep Melnick, *Between the Lines: Interpreting Welfare Rights* (Washington, D.C., 1994), p. 85.

41. *King v. Smith* at 320–27.

42. *Townsend v. Swank* 404 U.S. 282, 286 (1971), discussed in Melnick, *Between the Lines*, pp. 90–91.

43. 42 U.S.C. section 601 (1964 ed., supp. IV) quoted in *Dandridge v. Williams* 397 U.S. 471, 478, note 7 (1970), upholding the states' right to set their own standards of need, benefit levels, and maximum family grants. See also *Jefferson v. Hackney* 406 U.S. 535 (1972).

44. See Thomas Byrne Edsall and Mary D. Edsall, *Chain Reaction: The Impact of Race, Rights, and Taxes on American Politics* (New York, 1991), pp. 67–69, 106–7, describing the growing political potency of race-coded issues such as welfare during the late 1960s; Dan T. Carter, *The Politics of Rage: George Wallace, the Origins of the New Conservatism, and the Transformation of American Politics* (New York, 1995), chapter 12, discussing the use of welfare to race-bait policymakers and voters; and Jill Quadagno, *The Color of Welfare: How Racism Undermined the War on Poverty* (New York, 1994), analyzing the racially contested democratization of social policy during the 1960s and early 1970s.

45. U.S. Senate, Committee on Finance, *Hearings on H.R. 16311*, 91st Congress, 2d session (Washington, D.C., 1970), p. 407.

46. *Shapiro v. Thompson* 394 U.S. 618 (1969); *Goldberg v. Kelly* 397 U.S. 254 (1970).
47. *King v. Smith* at 316.
48. *Wyman v. James* 400 U.S. 309 (1971).
49. *Dandridge v. Williams*.
50. *Shapiro v. Thompson*.
51. *Lewis v. Martin* 397 U.S. 552 (1970).
52. *New Jersey Welfare Rights Organization et al. v. Cahill*, per curiam (1973).
53. *Van Lare v. Hurley* 421 U.S. 338 (1975).
54. *Barber v. Barber* 62 U.S. (21 How.) 582, 584 (1858) disclaimed federal judicial jurisdiction over divorce and alimony issues. *In re Burrus* 136 U.S. 586, 593–94 (1890) found that "the whole subject of the domestic relations of husband and wife, parent and child, belongs to the laws of the States and not to the laws of the United States." However, the domestic relations exception is not open-ended; see *Ankenbrandt v. Richards* 112 S. Ct. 2206 (1992), which limits the exception to alimony, divorce, and child custody decrees.
55. *Goldberg v. Kelly* at 266.
56. *Goldberg v. Kelly* at 262, note 8.
57. Quoting from Charles Reich, "Individual Rights and Social Welfare: The Emerging Legal Issues," *Yale Law Journal* 74 (1965): 1245, 1255.
58. U. S. Senate, Committee on Finance, "Opening Statement of Senate Debate," H.R. 17550 (Social Security Amendments of 1970), December 14, 1970, pp. 76–77.
59. Daniel Patrick Moynihan, "Crisis in Welfare," reprinted in Moynihan, *Coping: Essays on the Practice of Government* (New York, 1973), pp. 151–54.
60. *Shapiro v. Thompson* at 630, 631.
61. *New York Department of Social Services v. Dublino* 413 U.S. 405 (1973).
62. E.g., *Doe v. Shapiro* 302 F. Supp. 761 (D. Conn. 1969); *Meyers v. Juras* 327 F. Supp. 759 (D. Ore. 1971); *Taylor v. Martin* 330 F. Supp. 85 (N.D. Cal. 1971); *Doe v. Flowers* 364 F. Supp. 953 (N.D. W. Va. 1973).
63. *Doe v. Shapiro* 764, quoted in *Doe v. Flowers* 955.
64. Quoted in Stephen D. Sugarman, "*Roe v. Norton*: Coerced Mater-

nal Cooperation," in *In the Interest of Children: Advocacy, Law Reform, and Public Policy*, ed. Robert H. Mnookin (New York, 1985), p. 409.

65. U. S. Senate, Committee on Finance, *Hearings on H.R. 1* (Social Security Amendments of 1971), 92$^d$ Congress, 1$^{st}$ session, (Washington, D.C., 1971), pp. 48–49.

66. Ibid., p. 184.

67. Vee Burke, "New Welfare Law: Comparison of the New Block Grant Program with Aid to Families with Dependent Children," *CRS Report for Congress*, August 26, 1996.

68. 42 U.S.C. section 601 (1988) (italics added).

69. States received waivers from the Bush and Clinton administrations to add various limitations to welfare eligibility. The Clinton administration had approved waivers for such initiatives as "wedfare" (bonuses for recipients who marry), "learnfare" (reduction or loss of benefits to familes with truant children) and time limits in thirty-five states by early 1996. Most popular were the family-cap/child-exclusion rules approved for some twenty states by 1996, which deny benefits to children born to mothers receiving welfare. Barbara Vobejda, "Most States Are Shaping Their Own Welfare Reform," *Washington Post*, February 3, 1996.

70. Robert Pear, "States Aren't Rewriting Book on Welfare Plans," *New York Times*, October 15, 1996; Children's Defense Fund, "Selected Features of State Welfare Plans" (CDF Update), November 13, 1996; Robert Pear, "Rewards and Penalties Vary in States' Welfare Programs," *New York Times*, February 23, 1997; Jason DeParle, "U. S. Welfare System Dies as State Programs Emerge," *New York Times*, June 30, 1997; Barbara Vobejda and Judith Havemann, "In Welfare Decisions, One Size No Longer Fits All," *Washington Post*, June 30, 1997; Virginia Ellis and Max Vanzi, "Legislature OKs Major Revamping of Welfare System," *Los Angeles Times*, August 5, 1997.

71. P.L. 104-193, Title I, section 402(a)(1)(A)(i).

72. Barbara Vobejda, "Will There Be a Race to the Bottom on Welfare?" *Washington Post National Weekly Edition*, September 18–24, 1995, p. 31.

73. P.L. 104-193, Title I, section 402. To be eligible for funds, a state must submit a plan indicating, among other things, how it intends to conduct its program; how it intends to require adult recipients to work outside the home not later than twenty-four cumulative months after first receiving assitance; how it intends to establish

goals and take action to reduce non-marital births; how it intends to provide education and training about statutory rape; that it will run a child support enforcement program; that it will run a foster care and adoption assistance program; and that it will prevent fraud.

74. Ibid., section 402(a)(1)(v).

75. Ibid., section 403(a)(2). The 1997 Balanced Budget Act provides that bonuses be awarded to states based on reduced ratios of non-marital births to all births ("illegitimacy ratio") rather than on reduced numbers of non-marital births. This advantages states with increasing marital birthrates. U.S. House of Representatives, *H. R. 2015*, Title V, subtitle F, chapter 1, section 5502 (b).

76. Timothy Egan, "Take This Bribe, Please, for Values to Be Received," *New York Times*, November 12, 1995.

77. P.L. 104-193, Title I, section 408(a)(5), (8).

78. Ibid., section 408(a)(4), (5).

79. Ibid., section 488(a)(7).

80. Marcia Coyle and Harvey Berkman, "Welfare Entitlements Face Erosion: Cash-strapped Advocates Will Face State Court Patchwork in Absence of Federal Regs," *National Law Journal*, June 17, 1996.

81. *United States v. Lopez* 115 S. Ct. 1624 (1995). The majority wrote: "Under the Government's 'national productivity' reasoning, Congress could regulate any activity that it found was related to the economic productivity of individual citizens: family law (including marriage, divorce, and child custody), for example. Under the theories that the Government presents . . . it is difficult to perceive any limitation on federal power, even in areas such as criminal law enforcement or education where States historically have been sovereign. Thus if we were to accept the Government's arguments, we are hard-pressed to posit any activity by an individual that Congress is without power to regulate."

82. P.L.104-193, Title I, sections 101, 401.

## Chapter 3. Disdained Mothers, Unequal Citizens

1. P.L. 104-193, Title I, section 408(a)(5).

2. Tom Bethell, "Roe's Disparate Impact: Why Abortion's Not Just for Catholics Anymore," *Human Life Review* 22 (Summer 1996):

114; Tamar Lewin, "Abortion Foes Worry about Welfare Cutoffs," *New York Times,* March 19, 1995; Leslie Albrecht Popiel, "Critics See Welfare Reform Increasing U. S. Abortion Rate," *Christian Science Monitor,* July 22, 1994.

3. P.L. 104-193, Title I, section 403(a)(2).

4. *Eisenstadt v. Baird* 405 U.S. 438 (1972).

5. *Levy v. Louisiana* 391 U.S. 68 (1968) found it "invidious to discriminate" between marital and non-marital children; *Gomez v. Perez* 409 U.S. 535 (1973) and *Mills v. Habluetzel* 456 U.S. 91 (1982) both held that if a state grants opportunity to marital children to obtain parental support it must also do so for non-marital children.

6. *Weber v. Aetna Casualty* 406 U.S. 164, 173 (1971).

7. *Trimble v. Gordon* 430 U.S. 762 (1977); *Reed v. Campbell* 476 U.S. 852 (1986).

8. *New Jersey Welfare Rights Organization et al. v. Cahill* 411 U.S. 619 (1973).

9. P.L. 104-193, Title III, subtitle D, section 333; Title I, section 408(a)(2).

10. P.L. 104-193, Title III, subtitle D, section 333(3); Title I, section 402(7)(A)(iii); Jody Raphael, "Domestic Violence and Welfare Receipt: Toward a New Feminist Theory of Welfare Dependency," *Harvard Women's Law Journal* 19 (Spring 1996): 222; Nina Siegal and Martin Espinoza, "No Escape: How Welfare and Immigration Reform Will Keep Battered Women Prisoners of Abuse," *San Francisco Bay Guardian,* April 30–May 6, 1997, pp. 17–23.

11. *King v. Smith* 392 U.S. 309 (1968), at 329, found "it beyond reason to believe that Congress would have considered that providing employment for the paramour of a deserted mother would benefit the mother's children whom he was not obligated to support."

12. P.L. 104-193, Title I, section 408(a)(2).

13. Vicki Turetsky, Senior Staff Attorney, Center for Law and Social Policy, "Penalty on Families without Established Paternity," testimony submitted to the U. S. House of Representatives, Committee on Ways and Means, Subcommittee on Human Resources, June 13, 1995.

14. Peter Kilborn, "Welfare Mothers Losing Bonus They Got to Help Track Fathers," *New York Times,* November 12, 1996. States may continue to pass $50 from monthly child support collections to mothers, but may not use federal funds to do so. As of May 1997,

twenty-five states had decided to stop paying a pass-through. Eight states were uncertain about what they would do. Seventeen states had decided to continue some type of pass-through. Vicki Turetsky and Andrea Watson, Center for Law and Social Policy, "Some States Continue $50 Child Support Pass-through Despite Federal Disincentive," June 1997.

15. *Blessing v. Freestone* 1997 WL 188396 (U. S.). Although the case was brought under the Family Support Act of 1988, the Court ruled that its reasoning applied to the 1996 Personal Responsibility Act as well.

16. P.L. 104-193, Title I, section 408(a)(2),(3); Title III, subtitle A, section 301(a), subtitle D, section 333.

17. Ibid., Title III, subtitle G, sections 361, 365.

18. Paul Valentine, "Maryland Suspends Licenses over Child Support: Thousands of Parents Lose the Right to Drive," *Washington Post*, February 5, 1997.

19. P.L. 104-193, Title III, subtitle G, section 370.

20. Raphael, "Domestic Violence and Welfare Receipt," p. 222. A recent study showed very high rates of domestic violence suffered by mothers on welfare, particularly among those engaged in conflicts with fathers over custody, visitation, and child support. Randy Albeda, et al., "In Harm's Way? Domestic Violence, AFDC Receipt and Welfare Reform in Massachusetts," Center for Social Policy Research and the McCormack Institute (Boston, 1997). On the problems created for women's equality by private violence, see Brande Stellings, "The Public Harm of Private Violence: Rape, Sex Discrimination, and Citizenship," *Harvard Civil Rights–Civil Liberties Law Review* 28 (Winter 1993): 185–216.

21. Following the Uniform Parentage Act's "presumption of legitimacy," most states automatically assign paternity to husbands of women who bear children in marriages.

22. *Douglas v. Babcock* 990 F. 2d 875 (1993) (*cert. denied, Douglas v. Miller* 510 U.S. 825).

23. *Sherbert v. Verner* 374 U.S. 398 (1963); *Shapiro v. Thompson* 394 U.S. 618 (1969).

24. Lynn A. Baker, "The Prices of Rights: Toward a Positive Theory of Unconstitutional Conditions," *Cornell Law Review* 75 (1990): 1185–1257.

25. For two fascinating windows onto paternity establishment, see

Renee A. Monson, "State-ing Sex and Gender: Collecting Information from Mothers and Fathers in Paternity Cases," *Gender and Society* 11 (June 1997): 279–96, and Lisa Kelly, "If Anybody Asks You Who I Am: An Outsider's Story of the Duty to Establish Paternity," *Yale Journal of Law and Feminism* 6 (Summer 1994): 297–305.

26. However, one study in Cuyahoga County, Ohio, measured high rates (45 percent) of noncooperation among custodial mothers receiving welfare. Charles Adams, Jr., David Landsbergen, and Larry Cobler, "Welfare Reform and Paternity Establishment: A Social Experiment," *Journal of Policy Analysis and Management* 11 (1992): 678.

27. Robert I. Lerman and Theodora J. Ooms, "Unwed Fathers," *American Enterprise,* September 1, 1993, pp. 30, 36.

28. William A. Galston, "A Liberal-Democratic Case for the Two-parent Family," *The Responsive Community* 1 (Winter 1990–91): 21.

29. Wilson's classic statement of this position is in *The Truly Disadvantaged* (Chicago, 1987).

30. William J. Eaton, "Shalala Revives 'Murphy Brown' Pregnancy Issue," *Los Angeles Times,* July 15, 1994.

31. Carolyn Lochhead, "Congresswomen Push to Make Fathers Pay: Bipartisan Proposal Would Make It Harder to Evade Child Support," *San Francisco Chronicle,* June 9, 1994; Rhonda McMillion, "Child Support Enforcement Gets a Boost," *ABA Journal* 80 (September 1994): 87.

32. Harry D. Krause, "Child Support Reassessed: Limits of Private Responsibility and the Public Interest," *Family Law Quarterly* 24 (Spring 1990): 17.

33. David Blankenhorn, *Fatherless in America* (New York, 1995), p. 25.

34. David Popenoe, "A World without Fathers," *Wilson Quarterly* 20 (Spring 1996): 21.

35. George Gilder, *Wealth and Poverty* (New York, 1980).

36. Charles Murray, "The Coming White Underclass," *Wall Street Journal,* October, 1993. Murray fired his opening shot against welfare in his 1984 *Losing Ground: American Social Policy, 1950–1980.* For a critical assessment of Murray's welfare politics, see Theodore J. Lowi and Gwendolyn Mink, "Charles Murray: Losing Ground, Gaining Power," in *Required Reading: Sociology's Most Influential Books,* ed. Dan Clawson (Amherst, Mass., forthcoming).

37. Linda Feldmann, "Unwed Parents: Seeking Answer to Teen Moms, Some Experts Suggest End to Aid," *Christian Science Monitor*, May 27, 1994.

38. Barbara Vobejda, "Gauging Welfare's Role in Motherhood," *Washington Post*, June 2, 1994.

39. Quoted in Linda McClain, "'Irresponsible Reproduction'," *Hastings Law Journal* 47 (January 1996): 388.

40. "Single Women and Poverty Strongly Linked," *New York Times*, February 20, 1994.

41. Elizabeth Thomson, Thomas L. Hanson, and Sara S. McLanahan, "Family Structure and Child Well-being: Economic Resources vs. Parental Behaviors," *Social Forces* 73 (September 1994): 221ff. Sara McLanahan, "The Consequences of Single Motherhood," *American Prospect* no. 18 (Summer 1994): 48ff.

42. For a discussion of liberal family values rhetoric, see Iris Marion Young, "Making Single Motherhood Normal," *Dissent* 41 (Winter 1994): 88–93.

43. Barbara Vobejda, "Status of Child Support Called 'Shameful'," *Washington Post*, May 14, 1995.

44. On the importance of a paternity-based child support policy for gender and equality, see Susan Moller Okin, *Justice, Gender, and the Family* (New York, 1989), pp. 175–78.

45. Katha Pollitt, "Subject to Debate," *The Nation*, January 30, 1995, p. 120.

46. See, e.g., "Remarks of Mrs. Kennelly," *Congressional Record*, January 31, 1995, p. H895; "Remarks of Mrs. Woolsey," *Congressional Record*, February 1, 1995, p. H1031.

47. "Statement of Ms. Elizabeth C. Spalding of Greenwich, Conn., and Betty Berry of New York City in Behalf of the National Organization for Women," *Hearings on Child Support and the Work Bonus*, S. 2081, U. S. Senate, Committee on Finance, 93ᵈ Congress, 1ˢᵗ session, September 25, 1973, pp. 176–201; "Statement of Mrs. Kenneth Greenawalt, National Human Resources Chairman, League of Women Voters," ibid., pp. 212–18.

48. Ellen Goodman, "Throwing the Book at Delinquent Fathers," *Los Angeles Times*, November 9, 1983; Mary Frances Berry, *The Politics of Parenthood: Child Care, Women's Rights, and the Myth of the Good Mother* (New York, 1993), pp. 153, 157.

49. Paul K. Legler, "The Coming Revolution in Child Support Policy:

Implications of the 1996 Welfare Act," *Family Law Quarterly* 30 (Fall 1996): 524.

50. E.g., "The Interstate Child Support Enforcement Act," H.R. 95, introduced by Congresswoman Barbara Kennelly (D-Connecticut) in January, 1995. The bill provided for direct withholding of wages from deadbeat dads and other penalties contained in the Republican welfare bill. It also called for seizing lottery winnings and awards, attaching bank accounts, attaching private and public pension funds, putting liens on certificates of vehicle title, and denying vehicle registration.

51. Congresswoman Lynn Woolsey, "Remarks," in *Women and Welfare Reform: Women's Poverty, Women's Opportunities, and Women's Welfare*, ed. Gwendolyn Mink, Conference Proceedings, Institute for Women's Policy Research, October 23, 1993.

52. "Remarks of Mrs. Woolsey," *Congressional Record*, February 1, 1995, p. H1031. Woolsey's experience received attention again when she and Congressman Henry Hyde (R-Illinois) introduced legislation to turn child support collection over to the Internal Revenue Service. Adam Clymer, "Child Support Collection Net Usually Fails," *New York Times*, July 17, 1997.

53. Ellen L. Bassuk, Angela Browne, and John C. Buckner, "Single Mothers and Welfare," *Scientific American*, October 1996, p. 62.

54. Krause, "Child Support Reassessed," p. 13.

55. On the "implicit stories of race and gender" in welfare politics, see Nancy E. Dowd, "Stigmatizing Single Parents," *Harvard Women's Law Journal* 18 (1995): 19, 26, 45–46; Regina Austin, "Sapphire! Bound," *University of Wisconsin Law Review* (1989), reprinted in *Feminist Jurisprudence*, ed. Patricia Smith (New York, 1993), pp. 575–94; Martha Fineman, *The Neutered Mother, the Sexual Family* (New York, 1995), chapter 5.

56. U. S. House of Representatives, Committee on Ways and Means, *1996 Green Book* (Washington, D.C., 1996), p. 516, chart 8-5. Forty-five percent of AFDC spells began as a result of divorce or marital separation, as compared to 30 percent of spells precipitated by non-marital births. McClain, "'Irresponsible Reproduction'," p. 356, note 61.

57. U. S. House of Representatives, *1996 Green Book*, chart 8-6.

58. In 1994, care-givers who received benefits under AFDC were: 37.4 percent white; 36.4 percent Black; 19.9 percent Latina; 2.9

percent Asian; 1.3 percent Native American. U. S. House of Representatives, *1996 Green Book*, p. 480. A Yale University study recently showed a powerful association between race and popular
representations of poverty. Although 29 percent of Americans below the poverty line are Black, national news magazines pictured
Blacks 62 percent of the time in stories on poverty and evening
television news did so 65 percent of the time. "Study: Media Por-
trays Poor as Black," Associated Press, August 19, 1997.

59. Ibid., Table 8-2.

60. Joan Sylvain, *"Michael H. v. Gerald D.:* The Presumption of Paternity," *Catholic University Law Review* 39 (1990): 831–58.

61. Jessica Delgado and Kereth Frankel Klein, "In the Matter of . . .
Dana S. and Marcie J. vs. Jefferson S.," moot court brief, University
of California, Boalt Hall School of Law, April 1996. See also Roger
J. R. Levesque, "The Role of Unwed Fathers in Welfare Law: Failing Legislative Initiatives and Surrendering Judicial Responsibility," *Law and Inequality: A Journal of Theory and Practice* 12 (December 1993): 93–126.

62. *Lehr v. Robertson* 463 U.S. 248 (1983) found that a non-marital
biological father who had never supported and had rarely seen his
child did not enjoy due process rights to participate in an adoption
decision.

63. Ibid. at 256, 261–62. See also *Parham v. Hughes* 441 U.S. 347 (1979),
which upheld a Georgia statute precluding a non-marital biological father who had not legitimated his child from suing for the
child's wrongful death.

64. *Michael H. v. Gerald D.* 491 U.S. 110 (1988).

65. Ibid. at 118–19.

66. P.L. 104-193, Title III, subtitle F; subtitle G, section 365(a)(15)
(A)(ii), sections 367–70.

67. Ibid., Title III, subtitle I, section 469B(a).

68. Daniel Patrick Moynihan, *Family and Nation* (New York, 1986),
pp. 180–81.

69. Thom Weidlich, "Dad's Rights Advocates Come of Age: Once an
Angry Fringe, Now They Target Custody, Welfare, and Child Support Laws," *National Law Journal*, March 13, 1995.

70. Amy E. Hirsch, "Income Deeming in the AFDC Program: Using
Dual Track Family Law to Make Poor Women Poorer," *Review of
Law and Social Change* 16 (1987–88): 725.

71. *Quilloin v. Walcott* 434 U.S. 246 (1978); *Michael H. v. Gerald D.*
72. *Mills v. Habluetzel* 102 S. Ct. 1549, 1558, n. 4 (1982) struck down a Texas law requiring that for child support purposes, the paternity of a non-marital child must be established before the child is one year old: "The unwillingness of the mother to file a paternity action on behalf of her child, which could stem from her relationship with the natural father or even from the desire to avoid community and family disapproval, may continue years after the child is born." *Clark v. Jeter* 486 U.S. 456 (1987) invalidated Pennsylvania's six-year statute of limitations for paternity establishment.
73. *Meyer v. Nebraska* 262 U.S. 390 (1923); *Pierce v. Society of Sisters* 268 U.S. 510 (1925); *Prince v. Massachusetts* 321 U.S. 158 (1944); *Wisconsin v. Yoder* 406 U.S. 205 (1972); *Stanley v. Illinois* 405 U.S. 645 (1972); *Cleveland Board of Education v. LaFleur* 414 U.S. 632 (1974); *Moore v. City of East Cleveland, Ohio* 431 U.S. 494 (1976).
74. *Prince v. Massachusetts* at 166.
75. *Moore v. City of East Cleveland.*
76. *Stanley v. Illinois.*
77. *Meyer v. Nebraska, Pierce v. Society of Sisters,* and *Wisconsin v. Yoder.*
78. *M.L.B. v. S.L.J.* 95-853 (December 16, 1996), 12.
79. *Loving v. Virginia* 388 U.S. 1, 12 (1967), citing *Skinner v. Oklahoma* 316 U.S. 535, 541 (1942).
80. *United States v. Kras* 409 U.S. 434, 444 (1973).
81. *Zablocki v. Redhail* 434 U.S. 374 (1977), struck down a Wisconsin statute that persons who have not met their child support obligations may not marry, until the obligation has been met and absent a showing that children covered by the support order "are not then and are not likely thereafter to become public charges."
82. *Griswold v. Connecticut* 381 U.S. 479, 495 (1965).
83. *Eisenstadt v. Baird* 405 U.S. 438, 453–54 (1972).
84. *Roe v. Wade* 410 U.S. 113 (1973).
85. Feminists challenged the child exclusion (family cap) on these grounds in *C.K. v. Shalala* 92 F. 3d 171 (1996). The U. S. Court of Appeals for the Third Circuit found that New Jersey's child exclusion policy did not unduly burden procreative choice, since "it in no way conditions receipt of benefits upon plaintiffs' reproductive choices," at 194. The NOW–Legal Defense and Education Fund argued the case for recipients harmed by the policy. They were joined by a slew of women's groups as *amici curiae,* including the

National Organization for Women, the National Abortion and Reproductive Rights Action League, and the Fund for a Feminist Majority.

86. Spenser S. Hsu, "Welfare Law in Va. Awakens a Past Horror," *Washington Post*, February 8, 1996.

87. Kelly, "If Anybody Asks You Who I Am," pp. 303–4.

88. Marcia Coyle and Harvey Berkman, "Welfare Entitlements Face Erosion," *National Law Journal*, June 17, 1996, p. 8, discussing *Doe v. Gallant* 96-01307 (Super. Ct., Suffolk County, Massachusetts).

89. *Tomas v. Rubin* 926 F. 2d 906 (1991).

90. *Relf et al. v. Weinberger* 372 F. Supp. 1196 (1974); *Relf et al. v. Mathews* 403 F. Supp. 1235 (1975); *Relf et al. v. Weinberger* 565 F. 2d 722 (1977).

91. Donald Kimelman, "Poverty and Norplant: Can Contraception Reduce the Underclass?" *Philadelphia Inquirer*, December 12, 1990.

92. "Birth-control Implant Gains among the Poor," *New York Times*, December 17, 1992; Barbara Katrowitz and Pat Wingert, "The Norplant Debate," *Newsweek*, February 15, 1993, pp. 37–42; David S. Coale, "Norplant Bonuses and the Unconstitutional Conditions Doctrine," *Texas Law Review* 71 (1992): 189–215.

93. *Maher v. Doe* 432 U.S. 464 (1977); *Harris v. McRae* 448 U.S. 297 (1980).

94. P.L. 104-193, Title IX, section 912.

95. *Buck v. Bell* 274 U.S. 200 (1927).

96. Stephen Jay Gould, "Carrie Buck's Daughter," *Natural History* 93 (July 1984).

97. *Buck v. Bell* at 206.

98. Dorothy Roberts makes a parallel point in "The Only Good Poor Woman: Unconstitutional Conditions and Welfare," *Denver University Law Review* 72 (1995): 945.

99. Lewin, "Abortion Foes Worry about Welfare Cutoffs."

## Chapter 4. Why Should Poor Single Mothers Have to Work Outside the Home?

1. P.L. 104-193, Title I, section 402 (a)(1)(B)(iv).

2. Ibid., section 407 (a)(1). The PRA approves the following twelve "work activities": (1) unsubsidized employment; (2) subsidized

private sector employment; (3) subsidized public sector employment; (4) work experience, including work associated with the refurbishing of publicly assisted housing, if sufficient private sector employment is not available; (5) on-the-job training; (6) job search and job readiness assistance; (7) community service programs; (8) vocational educational training (not to exceed twelve months); (9) job skills training directly related to employment; (10) education directly related to employment, in the case of a recipient who has not received a high school diploma or a certificate of high school equivalency; (11) satisfactory attendance at secondary school or in studies for a GED (general equivalency degree), for a recipient who has not received a high school diploma or its equivalent; and (12) the provision of child care services to an individual who is participating in a community service program.

3. Ibid., section 407 (e)(1).

4. Ibid., section 409 (3). A state that doesn't meet its work participation rates loses 5 percent of its TANF block grant the first year, 7 percent the next year, then 9 percent the following year—up to a maximum penalty of 21 percent. U. S. House of Representatives, Committee on Ways and Means, *1996 Green Book* (Washington, D.C., 1996), p. 1335.

5. P.L. 104-193, Title I, section 402 (a)(1)(B)(iv).

6. Ibid., section 407 (b)(5).

7. Ibid., section 407 (e)(2).

8. On the contradictory and problematic development of work requirements, see Sylvia Law, "Women, Work, Welfare, and the Preservation of Patriarchy," *University of Pennsylvania Law Review* 131 (1983): 1249–1339.

9. P.L. 104-193, Title I, section 401 (4).

10. Ibid., section 407 (c)(1)(B).

11. Heidi Hartmann, Roberta Spalter-Roth, and Jacqueline Chu, "Poverty Alleviation and Single-mother Families," *Phi Kappa Phi Journal* (Summer 1996): 24; Roberta M. Spalter-Roth and Heidi Hartmann, "AFDC Recipients as Care-givers and Workers: A Feminist Approach to Income Security Policy for American Women," *Social Politics* 1 (Summer 1994): 192; "Annual Update of the HHS Poverty Guidelines," *Federal Register*, vol. 62 (March 10, 1997), p. 10857.

12. U. S. Department of Labor, Women's Bureau, *1993 Handbook on Women Workers: Trends and Issues* (Washington, D.C., 1994).

13. Joe Klein, "Clintons on the Brain," *The New Yorker,* March 17, 1997, p. 62.

14. A single mother with a child under age six meets the work test if she works outside the home at least twenty hours per week. P.L. 104-193, Title I, section 407 (c)(2)(B).

15. *Merriam-Webster's Collegiate Dictionary,* 10th ed. (Springfield, Mass., 1996), s.v. "¹work."

16. P.L. 104-193, Title I, section 407 (d)(12).

17. Peter T. Kilborn, "Child-care Solutions in a New World of Welfare," *New York Times,* June 1, 1997.

18. P.L. 104-193, Title I, section 407 (d)(7).

19. For some recipients' descriptions of their dead-end work assignments under the Family Support Act, see Julia Teresa Quiroz and Regina Tosca, *For My Children: Mexican American Women, Work, and Welfare* (Washington, D.C., 1992), pp. 10–13.

20. David Riemer, "Welfare Recipients Need Wages, Not Workfare," *New York Times,* December 30, 1996. In the 105th Congress, Representative Patsy Mink (D-Hawaii) introduced House Resolution 1045 to give economic value to the unremunerated work performed by welfare recipients and to define that economic value as "earned income" for EITC purposes.

21. P.L. 104-193, Title I, section 407(f)(2).

22. Bettina Boxall, "How Fair Is Workfare?" *Los Angeles Times,* March 9, 1997.

23. Marc Cooper, "When Push Comes to Shove: Who Is Welfare Reform Really Helping?" *The Nation,* June 2, 1997, pp. 11–15.

24. Jason DeParle, "White House Calls for Minimum Wage in Workfare Plan," *New York Times,* May 16, 1997; U. S. Department of Labor, "How Workplace Laws Apply to Welfare Recipients" (Washington, D.C., May 1997).

25. Robert Pear, "GOP Backing Off a Deal to Restore Aid to Immigrants," *New York Times,* June 5, 1997; Robert Pear, "Republican Leaders Exempt 'Workfare' from Labor Laws," *New York Times,* July 19, 1997.

26. "Gingrich: More Welfare Reform on GOP Agenda," August 3, 1997, http://allpolitics.com/1997/08/02/newt.interview/; Laura

Meckler, "GOP Vows to Fight over Welfare Work," Associated Press, July 29, 1997.

27. Louis Uchitelle, "Welfare Recipients Taking Jobs Often Held by the Working Poor," *New York Times,* April 1, 1997; Leslie Kaufman, "Welfare's Labor Pains: Old Style Union Organizers Battle over 'Workfare'," *Newsweek,* March 31, 1997, p. 39.

28. Cooper, "When Push Comes to Shove," p. 12.

29. Steven Greenhouse, "Nonprofit and Religious Groups to Fight Workfare in New York," *New York Times,* July 24, 1997.

30. Spalter-Roth and Hartmann, "AFDC Recipients as Care-givers and Workers," p. 197; W. Ann Reynolds, "For Students on Welfare, Degrees Pay Dividends," *Chronicle of Higher Education,* March 21, 1997, p. A68.

31. A full-year, full-time minimum wage worker earns $10,712.

32. Carla Rivera, "Welfare Law's Job Goal May Be Impossible," *Los Angeles Times,* November 4, 1996.

33. Spalter-Roth and Hartmann, "AFDC Recipients as Care-givers and Workers," p. 197.

34. Margaret G. Brooks and John C. Buckner, "Work and Welfare: Job Histories, Barriers to Employment, and Predictors of Work among Low-income Single Mothers," *American Journal of Orthopsychiatry* 66 (October 1996): 526–37.

35. Kathryn Edin and Laura Lein, *Making Ends Meet* (New York, 1997), discussed by Jason DeParle, "Learning Poverty Firsthand," *New York Times Magazine,* April 27, 1997, p. 34.

36. Peter Edelman, "The Worst Thing Bill Clinton Has Done," *Atlantic Monthly,* March 1997, p. 52.

37. William J. Holstein and Warren Cohen, "Ready, Aim, Hire: Corporate America and Workfare as We Know It," *U. S. News and World Report,* March 31, 1997, pp. 48–51.

38. Harriet B. Presser and Amy G. Cox, "The Work Schedules of Low-educated American Women and Welfare," *Monthly Labor Review* 120 (April 1997): 25.

39. P.L. 104-193, Title VI, section 601; U. S. House of Representatives, *1996 Green Book,* p. 1337; P. Edelman, "The Worst Thing Bill Clinton Has Done," p. 50.

40. D.K. Seavey, *Back to Basics: Women's Poverty and Welfare Reform* (Wellesley, Mass., 1996).

41. P.L. 104-193, Title I, section 402 (a)(7)(A)(iii); section 408 (a)(7)(C).

42. Jody Raphael, "Domestic Violence and Welfare Receipt: Toward a New Feminist Theory of Welfare Dependency," *Harvard Women's Law Journal* 19 (Spring 1996): 203, 205; Jennifer Gonnerman, "Welfare's Domestic Violence," *The Nation*, March 10, 1997, pp. 21–23.

43. Virginia Schein, *Working from the Margins: Voices of Mothers in Poverty* (Ithaca, N.Y., 1995), p. 42.

44. Hartmann, Spalter-Roth, and Chu, "Poverty Alleviation and Single Mother Families," p. 25; Kathleen Mullan Harris, "Life after Welfare. Women, Work, and Repeat Dependency," *American Sociological Review* 61 (June 1996): 408.

45. Schein, *Working from the Margins*, p. 43.

46. Ibid., p. 29.

47. Charles Murray, *Losing Ground: American Social Policy, 1950–1980* (New York, 1984).

48. Michael Tanner, Stephen Moore, and David Hartman, "Welfare Pays Better, So Why Work?" *USA Today*, March 1997, pp. 22–24.

49. Howard V. Hayghe and Suzanne M. Bianchi, "Married Mothers' Work Patterns: The Job-family Compromise," *Monthly Labor Review* 117 (June 1994): 25, table 1.

50. Ibid., pp. 26–27, tables 3 and 4.

51. Ibid., p. 28, table 5.

52. Ibid., p. 25, table 2.

53. U. S. House of Representatives, *1996 Green Book*, p. 480, table 8-32.

54. Sandra Blakeslee, "Studies Show Talking with Infants Shapes Basis of Ability to Think," *New York Times*, April 17, 1997.

55. Klein, "Clintons on the Brain," p. 62.

56. Bruce Reed, quoted by Klein, "Clintons on the Brain," p. 62.

57. Blakeslee, "Talking with Infants."

58. Nina Bernstein, "Deletion of Word in Welfare Bill Opens Foster Care to Big Business," *New York Times*, May 4, 1997.

59. Louise Armstrong, *Of 'Sluts and Bastards': A Feminist Decodes the Child Welfare Debate* (Monroe, Me., 1995); Gwendolyn Mink, "Damned If They Do," *Women's Review of Books*, April 1996, pp. 18–19.

60. P.L. 105–89.

61. U. S. House of Representatives, Adoption and Safe Families Act of 1997. H.R. 867, Title II, Sec. 201, Sec. 473A, 105th Congress, 1st session.

62. Congresswoman Patsy Mink (D-Hawaii), *Congressional Record,* April 30, 1997, p. H2023.

63. *Weinberger v. Wiesenfeld* 95 S. Ct. 1225, 1230 (1975).

64. Ibid.

65. U. S. House of Representatives, Committee on Ways on Means, *Overview of Entitlement Programs: 1994 Green Book* (Washington, D.C., 1994), p. 35, table 1-15.

66. Social Security Administration, *Social Security Handbook,* 12th edition (Washington, D.C., 1995), sections 412, 418.

67. U. S. House of Representatives, *1996 Green Book,* p. 52, table 1-26.

68. Ibid., p. 24, p. 18, table 1-7C.

69. Peter T. Kilborn, "Welfare All over the Map," *New York Times,* December 8, 1996.

70. Recipients in high benefit states ($600 payment standard) were considered to have "worked their way off of welfare" when they had earned $820 a month for four months, or $790 a month for one year. Recipients in median benefits states ($400 payment standard) lost eligibility after earning $620 a month for four months, or $590 for one year. U. S. House of Representatives, 1996 Green Book, p. 392, table 8-2.

71. *Califano v. Boles* 443 U.S. 282, 289 (1979).

72. The Supreme Court in *Wiesenfeld* defined the purpose of survivors' insurance this way, p. 1230, note 10.

73. U. S. House of Representatives, "The Work and Responsibility Act of 1994," H.R. 4605, Titles I and II, 103rd Congress, 2nd session.

74. E.g., Paul Wellstone, "If Poverty Is the Question . . . ," *The Nation,* April 14, 1997, pp. 15–18.

75. E.g., Barbara Bergmann and Heidi Hartmann, "A Welfare Reform Based on Help for Working Parents," *Feminist Economics* 1 (Summer 1995): 85–89, and "Get Real! Look to the Future, Not the Past," in ibid., pp. 109–19.

76. Women's Committee of One Hundred, "Women's Pledge on Welfare Reform: Eliminating Poverty for Women and Their Children," Spring 1995 (author's files).

77. U. S. Department of Health, Education, and Welfare, *Work in America: Report of a Special Task Force to the Secretary of Health, Education, and Welfare* (Cambridge, Mass., 1973), pp. xix, 179.

78. Ibid., p. 65.

79. Ibid., p. 180.

80. U.S. House of Representatives, "Housing Opportunity and Responsibility Act of 1997," H.R. 2, Title I, section 105.

81. Congressman Joseph Kennedy, III (D-Massachusetts), *Congressional Record*, May 1, 1997, p. H2137.

## Chapter 5. After Welfare's End

1. Frances Fox Piven and Richard Cloward, *Regulating the Poor*, updated ed. (New York, 1993), pp. 346, 381, 395.

2. U.S. House of Representatives, Committee on Ways and Means, *2000 Green Book: Overview of Entitlement Programs*, 106th Congress, 2nd session (Washington, D.C., 2000), p. 1530.

3. U.S. Public Law 104-193, Title I, sec. 407(c)(1)(B); *2000 Green Book*, p. 357.

4. Joe Soss and Sanford Schram, "New Report Sows Confusion about Welfare, Poverty," *Women's Enews*, August 1, 2001.

5. P.L. 104-193, Title I, sec. 408(b).

6. State Policy Documentation Project, *Sanctions for Noncompliance with Work Activities* (June 6, 2001), http://www.spdp.org/tanf/sanctions/sanctions_findings.htm.

7. Robin M. Dion and LaDonna Pavetti, Mathematica Policy Research, *Access to and Participation in Medicaid and the Food Stamp Program* (Washington, D.C., 2000), pp. 15–17.

8. U.S. Department of Health and Human Services, Administration for Children and Families, *Temporary Assistance for Needy Families (TANF) Program: Third Annual Report to Congress* (Washington, D.C., August 2000), p. 115.

9. Jason DeParle, "Shrinking Welfare Rolls Leave Record High Share of Minorities," *New York Times*, July 24, 1998.

10. Elizabeth Lower-Basch, U.S. Department of Health and Human Services, Assistant Secretary for Planning and Evaluation, *"Leavers" and Diversion Studies: Preliminary Analysis of Racial Differences in Caseload Trends and Leaver Outcomes* (Washington, D.C., rev. December 2000).

11. *2000 Green Book*, p. 439, table 7-29.

12. U.S. Census Bureau, *Poverty in the United States, 1999* (Washington, D.C., 2000), table B-3.

13. U.S. Bureau of Labor Statistics, *Highlights of Women's Earnings in 1999*, Report 943 (Washington, D.C., 2000), charts 2 and 3.

14. *2000 Green Book*, pp. 1238, 1521.

15. Ibid., p. 1239, table G-4.

16. Ibid., p. 1246, table G-11.

17. Ibid., p. 1519.

18. U.S. Census Bureau, *Poverty Thresholds*, http://www.census. gov/hhes/poverty/threshld/thresh99.html.

19. Pamela Loprest, The Urban Institute, *How Are Families That Left Welfare Doing? A Comparison of Early and Recent Welfare Leavers* (Washington, D.C., April 2001); Yolanda Wu, "Why Welfare Recipients Need Access to Education, Training and High-Wage Occupations," National Council of Women's Organizations, Task Force on Economic Security, *Briefing* (Washington, D.C., July 27, 2001).

20. Women of Color Resource Center, *Working Hard, Staying Poor: Women and Children in the Wake of Welfare "Reform"* (Berkeley, Cal., 2000). On poverty in one state, see Donna Haig Friedman, Randy Albelda, Elaine Werby, and Michelle Kahan, *After Welfare Reform: Trends in Poverty and Emergency Service Use in Massachusetts* (Boston, 2001).

21. See, for example, Heather Boushey and Bethney Gundersen, Economic Policy Institute, *When Work Just Isn't Enough: Measuring Hardships Faced by Families after Moving from Welfare to Work* (Washington, D.C., 2001).

22. Harry Holzer and Michael Stoll, Public Policy Institute of California, *Employers and Welfare Recipients: The Effects of Welfare Reform in the Workplace* (Sacramento, Cal., 2001); Rebecca Gordon, Applied Research Center, *Cruel and Usual: How Welfare "Reform" Punishes Poor People* (Oakland, Cal., 2001).

23. U.S. Department of Health and Human Services, Assistant Secretary for Planning and Evaluation, *"Leavers" and Diversion Studies: Summary of Research on Welfare Outcomes Funded by ASPE* (Washington, D.C., 2000). On the impossibility of making ends meet on $7.00 an hour, see Barbara Ehrenreich, *Nickel and Dimed: On (Not) Getting By in America* (New York, 2001).

24. Lissa Bell and Carson Strege-Flora, National Campaign for Jobs and Income Support, *Access Denied* (Washington, D.C., 2000); U.S.

Department of Health and Human Services, *National Study of Child Care for Low-Income Families* (Washington, D.C., 1999).

25. Tamar Lewin, "Child Welfare Improves, U.S. Says," *New York Times*, July 19, 2001.

26. Wendell Primus and Robert Greenstein, *Analysis of Census Bureau's Income and Poverty Report for 1999* (Washington, D.C., 2000).

27. P.L. 105-33.

28. U.S. Department of Health and Human Services, *HHS's Fatherhood Initiative: Fact Sheet* (Washington, D.C., 2000).

29. U.S. Department of Health and Human Services, *HHS Fatherhood Initiative: Improving Opportunities for Low-Income Fathers* (Washington, D.C., 2000).

30. U.S. Department of Health and Human Services, Administration for Children and Families, Office of Family Assistance, *Helping Families Achieve Self-Sufficiency: Guide for Funding Services for Children and Families through the TANF Program* (Washington, D.C., 2000), pp. 3, 19; italics added.

31. NOW Legal Defense and Education Fund, "State Marriage Initiatives," Fact Sheet (June 2001).

32. *Federal Register*, vol. 65, no. 169 (Washington, D.C., August 2000), pp. 52815, 52819, 52838; 45 CFR, parts 265 and 270.

33. Robert Rector, "Implementing Welfare Reform and Restoring Marriage," in Stuart M. Butler and Kim R. Holmes, eds., Heritage Foundation, *Priorities for the President* (Washington, D.C., 2001) pp. 71–97.

34. Wade Horn, "Wedding Bell Blues: Marriage and Welfare Reform," *Brookings Review*, vol. 19, no. 3, (2001) pp. 39–42.

35. Ibid.

36. Andrew Bush and Wade Horn, Hudson Institute, *Fathers, Marriage and Welfare Reform* (1997), http://www.welfarereformer.org/articles/father.htm. In June 2001, during his Senate confirmation process, Horn distanced himself from his 1997 call to discriminate against single parents and non-marital children.

37. U.S. House of Representatives, H.R. 3073, *Fathers Count Act of 1999*, 106th Congress, 1st session (Washington, D.C., 1999), roll no. 586. As a measure of this bill's popularity, less than a month elapsed between its introduction and passage in the House.

38. U.S. House of Representatives, H.R. 4678, *Child Support Distribution Act of 2000*, 106th Congress, 2nd session (Washington, D.C., 2000), roll no. 457.

39. As the bill's title suggests, child support provisions were central to it. These included needed reforms to the child support system to permit or encourage states to pass through some child support collections to custodial parents enrolled in TANF and to convert some arrearages to custodial parents who have left TANF. Because of these child support provisions, some feminist groups—specifically, the National Women's Law Center—supported the bill (and more recent versions of it) notwithstanding its provisions regarding fatherhood and marriage. In addition, the Children's Defense Fund strongly supports the measure, using it as a criterion to rate members of the 106th Congress.

40. *Child Support Distribution Act of 2000*, Title V, subtitle B, sec. 511(c)(2)(c), 106th Congress, 2nd session (Washington, D.C., 2000).

41. U.S. House of Representatives, Committee on Ways and Means, *Child Support Distribution Act of 2000: Report to Accompany H.R. 4678*, 106th Congress, 2nd session (Washington, D.C., 2000), p. 17.

42. Ibid., p. 42.

43. *Child Support Distribution Act of 2000*, Title V, subtitle A, sec. 501(a) and 501(b).

44. Jennifer Hamer, *What It Means to Be Daddy: Fatherhood for Black Men Living Away from Their Children* (New York, 2001), pp. 124, 214.

45. D.C. Jobs Council, *Help Wanted: Low Income Job Seekers Assess the District of Columbia's One Stop Career Centers* (Washington, D.C., June 2001).

46. U.S. House of Representatives, H.R. 4671, *The Responsible Fatherhood Act of 2000*, 106th Congress, 2nd session (Washington, D.C., 2000).

47. U.S. House of Representatives, H.R. 1471, *Child Support Distribution Act of 2001*, 107th Congress, 1st session (Washington, D.C., 2001).

48. U.S. Senate, S. 685, *The Strengthening Working Families Act*, 107th Congress, 1st session (Washington, D.C., 2001).

49. Senator Evan Bayh, Floor Statement on the Confirmation of Wade Horn, U.S. Senate, *Congressional Record*, July 25, 2001, p. S8187.

50. U.S. Senate, S. 653, *Responsible Fatherhood Act of 2001*, 107th Congress, 1st session (Washington, D.C., 2001).

51. For example, Ron Haskins and Wendell Primus write, "As shown above, living in a female-headed family greatly increases a child's chances of living in poverty, especially if the female-headed family was created by a non-marital birth. Living in a married-couple family, in addition to reducing poverty, confers a host of other benefits on both children and adults. It follows that promoting marriage would be a good way to reduce child poverty." In "Welfare Reform and Poverty," *Welfare Reform and Beyond*, Brookings Institution, Policy Brief No. 4 (Washington, D.C., July 2001).

52. Women's Committee of 100, Project 2002, *An Immodest Proposal: Rewarding Women's Work to End Poverty* (2000), http://www.welfare2002.org.

53. Ann Crittenden Scott, "The Value of Housework: For Love or Money?" *Ms.* (July 1972), pp. 56–59.

54. U.S. Census Bureau, *Poverty Thresholds*, http://www.census.gov/hhes/poverty/threshld/thresh00.html.

55. A bill incorporating these changes has been introduced by Congressmember Patsy Mink (D-Hawaii) in the House of Representatives (H.R. 3113), with likely co-sponsorship by Senator Paul Wellstone (D-Minnesota) in the Senate. This discussion of TANF reforms is drawn from the Women's Committee of 100, "TANF Reform: Legislative Agenda," http://www.welfare2002.org; Congressmember Patsy Mink, "Dear Colleague: TANF Reform," July 31, 2001; the NOW-LDEF/BOB Coalition agenda for TANF reauthorization; and minutes of the ad hoc committee to develop the TANF reform bill, which includes Jacqueline Payne, Tim Casey, Sherry Liewant, and Yolanda Wu of NOW-LDEF and myself for the Women's Committee of 100 and for Representative Mink.

# Index

Tennessee, work requirements in,
62
Tenth Amendment, 54
Texas child support in, 162n.72;
time limits in, 63, 162n.72; welfare benefits in, 144n.24; work
requirements in, 62
Thirteenth Amendment, 6, 20, 27
Tillmon, Johnnie, 81
Tomas, Joy, 96
travel, right to, 14, 55, 57–58

Uniform Parentage Act, 88, 157n.21
United Airlines, jobs with, 113
United Parcel Service (UPS), jobs
with, 113
*United States v. Carolene Products*,
143n.17
*United States v. Kozminski*, 142–
43n.10, 147n.52
*United States v. Kras*, 94
*United States v. Lopez*, 66, 145n.30
universalism, effects of, 18, 84–85
UPS (United Parcel Service), jobs
with, 113
U.S. Children's Bureau, 151n.32
U.S. Congress: on child support,
87–88; on paternity establishment, 60, 81–82; on residency requirements, 57–58; responsibility
of, 16–17; states' restrictions supported by, 61–62; voucher
amendment in, 4; welfare consensus in, 2–3. *See also* Democratic Party; Republican Party
U.S. Constitution: on citizenship,
10; enforcement of, 16–17; on
equality, 16–17, 20, 54–55,
143n.17; on labor, 6, 20, 27; on
reproductive rights, 30–31; vs.
social rights, 12; on states'
rights, 54–55. *See also* Bill of
Rights; rights
U.S. Supreme Court: on AFDC-UF
program, 149n.15; on child support provisions, 73; on citizenship rights, 10–11; on coerced labor, 27, 142–43n.10; on
differential gender treatment, 17–
18; on family law and productivity; 66, 93–94, 145n.30; on funda-

mental rights, 76–77; on
government subsidy for exercis-
ing rights, 16; on illegitimacy, 71;
on marriage, 94; opposition to,
60; on paternity establishment,
58–59, 76, 88–90, 92–93; on residency requirements, 14, 55, 57–
58; on sexual and reproductive
rights, 94–95; on social provisions, 12; on states' vs. constitutional rights, 55–56; on welfare
rights, 14–15, 20–21, 53, 57,
142n.8. *See also King v. Smith*
Utah: adoption rewards in, 64;
time limits in, 63

veterans, entitlements for, 13
Virginia: non-marital childbearing
in, 100; paternity establishment
in, 95; welfare recipients as providers of child care in, 147n.50

wage work: attitudes toward, 9,
21, 24; availability of, 112–13,
138; challenges of, 116–17; equality in, 20, 138–39; expectations
for, 25–27, 41–43; gender discrimination in, 119–20, 137; imposition of, 6, 23–30, 41–42, 62–
63, 103; as legal obligation, 23–
30; moralistic push for, 23, 30,
34, 36–38, 105–7, 120; payment
for, 9, 112–13; privileging of, 2,
5, 26, 38–39; racism in, 24–25;
social problems related to, 129;
statistics on mothers in, 118–20;
as trigger for domestic violence,
114–15; welfare combined with,
116; women's right to, 23–24. *See
also* job training; work requirements; workers
Wallace, George, 22
War on Poverty, 22–23. *See also*
Great Society
wedfare, waiver on, 154n.69
*Weinberger v. Wiesenfeld*, 148n.59,
168n.72
welfare: context of, 1–2, 21–22, 84–
87, 115–16; definition of, 1–2, 51–
53, 105, 125, 135–39; effects of,
20–21, 103; end of, 63–67, 95–97,